THE PERILOUS JOURNEY OF
The Donner Party

THE PIONEER MONUMENT
AT DONNER LAKE

THE PERILOUS JOURNEY OF
The Donner Party

BY MARIAN CALABRO

CLARION BOOKS ꝏ NEW YORK

Clarion Books
a Houghton Mifflin Company imprint
215 Park Avenue South, New York, NY 10003
Copyright © 1999 by Marian Calabro

Book design by Sylvia Frezzolini Severance
The text is set in 13-point Bembo.

For information about permission
to reproduce selections from this book,
write to Permissions, Houghton Mifflin Company,
215 Park Avenue South, New York, NY 10003.

Printed in the U.S.A.

Library of Congress Cataloging-in-Publication Data
Calabro, Marian.
The perilous journey of the Donner party / by Marian Calabro.
        p.   cm.
Includes bibliographical references (p.   ) and index.
Summary: Uses materials from letters and diaries written by survivors of the Donner Party
to relate the experiences of that ill-fated group as they endured horrific circumstances on
their way to California in 1846–47.
ISBN 0-395-86610-3
1. Donner Party—Juvenile literature. 2. Pioneer children—West (U.S.)—History—
19th century—Juvenile literature. [1. Donner Party. 2. Overland journeys to the Pacific. 3. Survival.] I. Title.
F868.N   5C33   1999
979.4'03—dc21   98-29610
                                                                CIP
                                                                AC

        KPT   10 9 8 7 6 5 4 3 2

TO BERNIE

CONTENTS

ACKNOWLEDGMENTS

Deepest thanks to the Society of Children's Book Writers and Illustrators for the Anna Cross Giblin Nonfiction Research Grant, which greatly helped this book go from work-in-progress to published reality. To all the people who taught me so much about the Donner Party during my research trips in California and Nevada: descendants, librarians, teachers, trail hounds, museum docents, and historians (especially Kristin Johnson, who patiently answered many questions). To the invaluable Wednesday Night Writing Group—Marcia Savin, Beryl Afton, Wendy Matthews, and Nigel Pugh—and other writing friends who traveled the trail with me in words. To the public librarians of Bergen County, New Jersey, especially Nancy Fezell in Fair Lawn and everyone in Hasbrouck Heights. To Katherine Kirkpatrick, for her intrepid photo research on two coasts. To Sue Coil, publishing mentor and fellow writer, for years of encouragement. And to Dorothy Briley, for taking the chance.

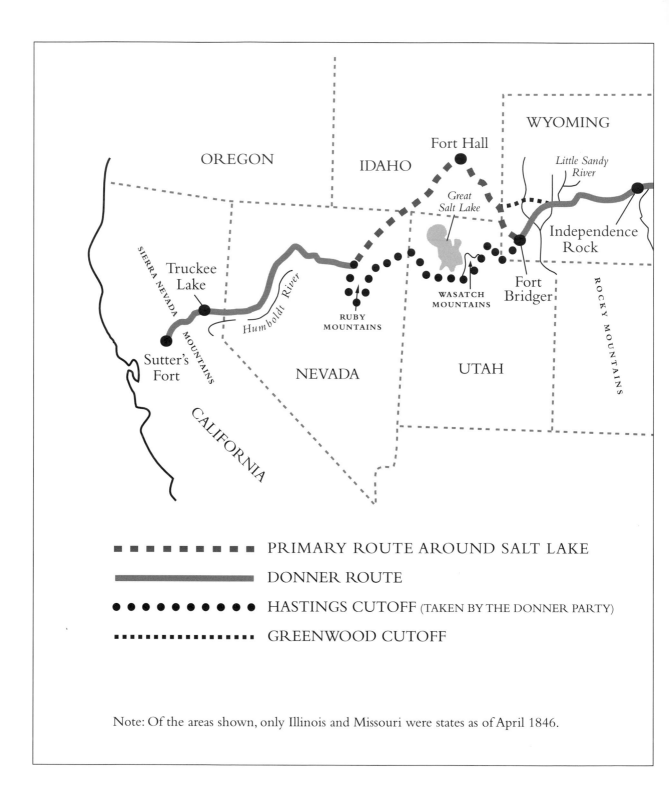

WYOMING

OREGON

Fort Hall

IDAHO

Little Sandy River

Great Salt Lake

Independence Rock

SIERRA NEVADA

Truckee Lake

Humboldt River

Fort Bridger

WASATCH MOUNTAINS

ROCKY MOUNTAINS

Sutter's Fort

MOUNTAINS

RUBY MOUNTAINS

NEVADA

UTAH

CALIFORNIA

■ ■ ■ ■ ■ ■ ■ PRIMARY ROUTE AROUND SALT LAKE

━━━━━━ DONNER ROUTE

● ● ● ● ● ● ● ● ● HASTINGS CUTOFF (TAKEN BY THE DONNER PARTY)

▪▪▪▪▪▪▪▪▪▪ GREENWOOD CUTOFF

Note: Of the areas shown, only Illinois and Missouri were states as of April 1846.

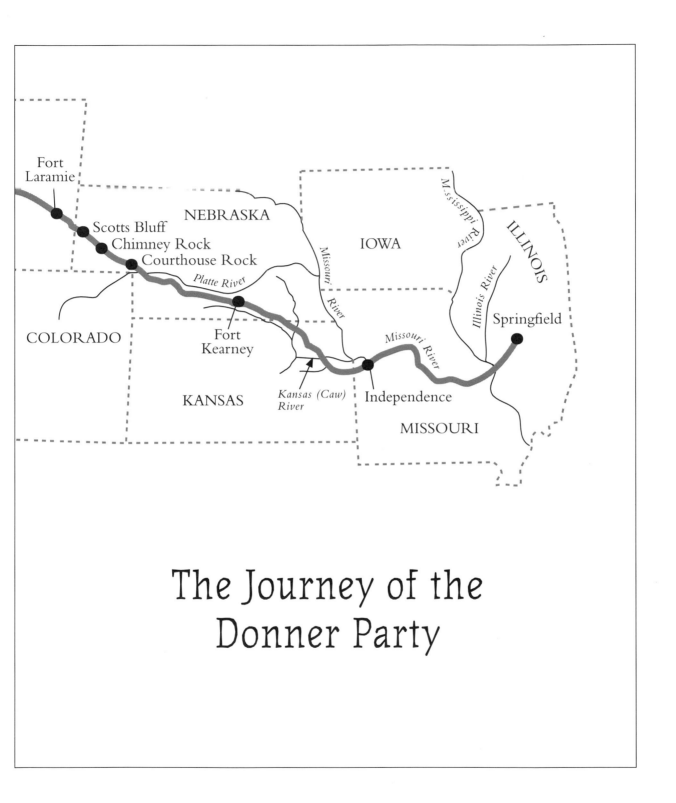

The Journey of the
Donner Party

MEMBERS OF THE DONNER PARTY

Names in parentheses are nicknames or alternate spellings. Numbers in parentheses are the approximate ages of the participants at the start of their journey. Question marks have been added to indicate ages particularly debated by historians.

These 32 people left from Springfield, Illinois, on April 15, 1846

Donner Families
George Donner (60?)
Tamsen (Tamzene) Eustis Dozier
  Donner, his wife (44)
Their children:
  Frances Eustis Donner (6)
  Georgia Ann Donner (4)
  Eliza Poor Donner (3)
George Donner's daughters from a
  previous marriage:
  Elitha Cumi Donner (14)
  Leanna Charity Donner (12)

Jacob Donner (56?), brother of George
Elizabeth (Betsy) Blue Hook Donner,
  his wife (45)

Their children:
  George Donner (9)
  Mary Donner (7)
  Isaac Donner (5)
  Samuel Donner (4)
  Lewis Donner (3)
Elizabeth Donner's sons from a
  previous marriage:
  Solomon Elijah Hook (14)
  William Hook (12)

Employees of the Donners
John Denton (28)
Noah James (20?)
Hiram Miller (28)—Miller left the
  Donner Party in July and is not usually

counted in the final tally of participants
Samuel Shoemaker (25?)

Reed Family
James Frazier Reed (45)
Margaret (Margret) Wilson Keyes
  Backenstoe Reed, his wife (32)
Their children:
  Martha Jane (Patty) Reed (8)
  James Frazier Reed Jr. (5)
  Thomas Keyes Reed (3)
Margaret Reed's daughter from a
  previous marriage:
  Virginia Elizabeth Backenstoe
  Reed (12)
Margaret Reed's mother:
  Sarah Hanley Keyes (70?)

Employees of the Reeds
Milford (Milt) Elliott (28)
Walter Herron (27)
James Smith (25?)
Baylis Williams (25?)
Eliza Williams (31), Baylis's half sister

These 59 people joined along the trail, between April and October 1846

Antonio (23, last name unknown),
  from New Mexico, employee of
  the Donners

Breen Family, from Iowa (recently immigrated from Ireland)
Patrick Breen (51)
Margaret Bulger Breen, his wife (36?)
Their children:
  John Breen (14)
  Edward Breen (13)

Patrick Breen Jr. (9)
Simon Preston Breen (8)
James Frederick Breen (5)
Peter Breen (3)
Margaret Isabella Breen (1)

Karl (Charles) Burger (30?), from
  Germany, employee of the Donners

Patrick Dolan (35?), from Ireland,
  friend of the Breens

Eddy Family, from Illinois
William Eddy (28)
Eleanor Priscilla Eddy, his wife (25)
Their children:
  James Eddy (3)
  Margaret Eddy (1)

Fosdick, *see under Graves Family*
Foster, *see under Murphy Family*

Graves Family, from Illinois
Franklin Ward Graves (57)
Elizabeth Cooper Graves, his wife (45)
Their children:
  Mary Ann Graves (19)
  William Cooper Graves (17)
  Eleanor (Ellen) Graves (14)
  Lovina Graves (12)
  Nancy Graves (9)
  Jonathan Graves (7)
  Franklin Ward Graves Jr. (5)
  Elizabeth Graves (1)
Also a married daughter and
  son-in-law:
  Jay Fosdick (23)
  Sarah Graves Fosdick (21)

Luke Halloran (25), from Missouri, traveling with the Donners

Mr. Hardcoop (first name unknown, 60?) from Belgium, traveling with the Kesebergs

Luis (age unknown), Native American (Miwok), employee of Sutter's Fort

Keseberg Family, from Germany
Johann Ludwig Christian (Louis) Keseberg (32)
Elisabeth Philippine Keseberg, his wife (23)
Their children:
    Ada Keseberg (3)
    Louis Keseberg Jr. (1)

McCutchen Family, from Missouri
William McCutchen (30)
Amanda Henderson McCutchen, his wife (25)
Their child:
    Harriet McCutchen (1)

Murphy Family, from Tennessee and Missouri
Levinah W. Jackson Murphy (36), widow
Her children:
    John Landrum Murphy (15)
    Meriam (Mary) M. Murphy (14)
    Lemuel B. Murphy (12)
    William Green Murphy (10)
    Simon Peter Murphy (8)
Also two married daughters and their families:
    William M. Foster (30)
    Sarah Ann Charlotte Murphy Foster (19)

Their child:
    George Foster (4?)
William M. Pike (25?)
Harriet Frances Murphy Pike (18)
Their children:
    Naomi Lavina Pike (2)
    Catherine Pike (1)

Pike, *see under Murphy family*

Joseph Reinhardt (30), from Germany, traveling with Augustus Spitzer

Salvador (age unknown), Native American (Miwok), employee of Sutter's Fort

John Snyder (25?), from Illinois, employee of the Graveses
Augustus Spitzer (30?), from Germany, traveling with Joseph Reinhardt

Charles Tyler Stanton (35), from Chicago, traveling with the Donners

Jean Baptiste Trudeau (16?), from New Mexico, employee of the Donners

Wolfinger, from Germany
Mr. Wolfinger (first name unknown, 30?)
Doris (20?), his wife

Springfield, Illinois, in the mid–1800s *(Library of Congress)*

Westward ho! Who wants to go to California without
it costing them anything? . . .
Come, Boys! You can have as much land as you want without costing
you any thing. The government of California gives large tracts of
land to persons who move there. The first suitable persons who
apply will be engaged.

—from a help-wanted ad placed by
George Donner in the *Sangamo Journal,* March 19, 1846

⟪⟫

CHAPTER 1
The Journey Begins

Virginia Elizabeth Backenstoe Reed, almost thirteen, sat on her horse and watched the last-minute frenzy all around her.

Springfield, Illinois, Virginia's hometown, was alive with people, horses, oxen, and covered wagons. The unpaved streets were muddy from spring rains. It was April 15, 1846, and three extended families, including Virginia's, were about to leave Springfield forever.

They had packed up everything they owned to move twenty-five hundred miles to a place they had never seen: California.

Life in Springfield wasn't bad. For well-off families like the Reeds, in fact, it was quite good. But California promised better things. It had already gotten Virginia a pony named Billy, a gift from her father to ride west on. "My pony was a perfect little beauty, cream collor with long heavey mane an[d] tail. Billy and I understood each other perfectly. I was in the habit of talking to him as though he was human." Virginia and her father would be the only people in the group riding horseback, rather than in the covered wagons, to California.

For months, Virginia's father and some acquaintances of his, George and Jacob Donner, had been talking about the lure of California, about how sunny, healthy, and fertile it would be. What really drew them, as Virginia probably knew, was free land.

James Frazier Reed and the Donner brothers, like so many people in the United States, had "land fever."

The particular land that attracted them was not theirs to take. California belonged to Mexico, as did much of the West. The land there was mostly empty. Oregon was drawing American pioneers, although it wasn't a formally organized territory yet. In spring 1846, the official United States extended only from the East Coast to Missouri and Texas. There were twenty-eight states in the Union.

But a mood was rising, a political movement, a belief that the nation must expand from ocean to ocean. "Manifest destiny," a recent newspaper editorial in New York City had grandly called it: "Our manifest destiny [is] to overspread and to possess the whole of the continent which Providence has given us, for the development of [our] great experiment of liberty. . . ."

The fact that Native Americans already possessed the West, by virtue of having lived there for thousands of years, was overlooked. Native Americans were regarded as inferiors or "savages" to be conquered. James Reed had already fought them in the Black Hawk War. He had served with another up-and-comer from Sangamon County, Illinois, a lawyer named Abraham Lincoln, a neighbor of the Reeds in Springfield.

The possibility of encountering hostile Indians on the way to California, or even the threat of war with Mexico, didn't scare Reed. Nor did it bother George Donner, the good-natured Springfield farmer who had placed the newspaper ad looking for hired hands to join the trip. ("As many as eight young men, of good character, who can drive an ox team, will be accommodated by gentlemen who will leave this vicinity about the first of April.") Hundreds of farm families, including some from Springfield, had safely made it to the West during the past three years. Reed and the Donners didn't want to miss out. California was particularly attractive because only a few hundred Americans lived there so far; plenty of free land was waiting.

Fifteen years before becoming
U.S. president, Abraham Lincoln
was a local lawyer and neighbor
of the Reeds in Springfield.
(Library of Congress)

Compared to today, little information about California was available in the way of travel planning. People relied mostly on hearsay, letters, and reports (often published in newspapers) that drifted back from the West. Basically, you went to Missouri—where the United States ended—and went on following the Oregon Trail until you turned left for California at a place called Fort Hall. Further advice came from travelers and trappers along the way.

However, James Reed and the Donner brothers had consulted a new book, *The Emigrants' Guide to Oregon and California,* which seemed to cover everything an emigrant needed to know. They weren't bothered that the author, Lansford Warren Hastings, didn't have a lot of experience on western trails. In 1846, one trip was enough to qualify you as an expert, at least in James Reed's eyes.

The Reeds and Donners expected to reach California's Sacramento Valley by autumn, especially if they took a new shortcut briefly described in Hastings's book. The way to succeed at the journey was to treat it as a race against time: The previous year, deep snows had closed the mountain passes into California the day after Christmas.

Facing west in flat Springfield, Virginia Reed probably imagined herself crossing those mountains. She had never actually seen mountains.

⌒᙭⌒

It couldn't have escaped Virginia's attention that some people in Springfield, including her own mother, questioned this move to California. Were the Donners being greedy? Was James Reed putting on airs? The fact that Reed had been born in Ireland of Polish ancestry, and that his real name was Reednowski, made some people uncomfortable. So did his big ambitions: Reed wanted to handle all U.S. government dealings with Native Americans west of the Rockies. Perhaps his fellow ex-soldier Abe Lincoln, soon to become a U.S. congressman, might help him with that.

James Reed was adventurous and competitive, and in their own way so were the Donners. George had already emigrated five times, starting from his birthplace of North Carolina. He was about sixty; Jacob was a few years younger. Both were widowed and remarried to younger wives. Between them, the brothers had twelve young children and stepchildren in their care. It was true that like many farmers, the Donners had been hit by recent depressions in crop prices. Yet both were prosperous. They knew the hardships of uprooting a household, and no doubt it would have been easier for them to stay put.

The same could be said of James Reed, who ran a successful mill and furniture-making business. A long, rough journey would be hard on his wife, Margaret. She suffered from "sick headaches" (possibly migraines), and no doubt was still mourning the recent death of a baby son. The move would be even riskier for Margaret's elderly mother, the bedridden Sarah Keyes, who lived with the Reeds and insisted on coming with them. The family had a nice house and servants. Would life in California really be better or even worth the disruption?

Success in the army and the furniture-making business had given James Reed a taste for fortune. Maybe, also, in his mid-forties, he had a sense of now or never. He never doubted the wisdom of moving west, and he took pains

James and Margaret Reed. A friend described James as "strong in his convictions, warm in his friendships, bitter in his hate; but honorable in apologizing if satisfied that he has been in the wrong." *(California State Parks, Sutter's Fort State Historical Park)*

to put Margaret at ease. "Several months were spent in preparing for the journey," Virginia later wrote. "Our wagons were made to order, that they might be strong and suitable for the trip."

The Reeds would travel as well as anyone could travel before trains existed or roads were paved. Few covered wagons were as comfortable as their main wagon, designed by James Reed, which would become known as the Pioneer Palace Car.

The palace car probably wasn't bigger than most family wagons, but it was a luxurious home on wheels. Many wagons forced riders to enter in the front, right behind the oxen, or to jump aboard in back. Reed had his builders put doors at the side, with a neat little set of portable steps. There were extensions over the wheels, upon which decking was laid. That expanded the usable space. And there was heat, thanks to a little wood stove with a chimney that poked through the canvas roof. "Mornings and evenings we could make a fire and warm the wagon up for Grandma," Virginia said.

To Virginia's eyes, the wagon's customized interior was as close to a living room as a wagon could be. There was space to carry sewing baskets, toys, and "a small library of select books, knowing such things were scarce in a new

A typical covered wagon interior. The Reeds' Pioneer Palace Car had even more room inside, with seats and built-in beds. *(National Archives)*

country." The bench seats in the middle of the wagon, called the parlor, were cushioned and set on springs, so, as Virginia said, "we could ride along and not be jolted to death" as the wagon moved forward on wooden wheels.

Beds were built in. The Reed children had a second-story loft for sleeping, while Grandma Keyes had a feather bed so she could travel in comfort despite being bedridden. The palace car even had a mirror inside, which must have made it feel even bigger.

Virginia understood the true reason for these luxuries. "Our wagon was so comfortable that mama could sit reading and chatting with the little ones and almost forget she was crossing the plains," she said. Her mother's work would be eased by the family's long-time servants, Baylis Williams and his half sister Eliza, who came along.

An artist's rendition of the Reeds' covered wagon on the plains, as later drawn for *Century* magazine, 1891 *(Author's Collection)*

Each of the three families had three wagons. One, like the Pioneer Palace Car, was to live in. The second carried daily supplies for the trip, mainly food, dishes, utensils, clothes, and tools. There was tallow (fat from sheep) to make candles and soap; rifles, gunpowder, lead, and shot—the men would be hunting along the way—and spare parts for the wagons.

The third wagon was like a moving van, full of things to be used in California: furniture, farm implements, fabric for new clothes, and dried food to carry them through their first winter. "We started with provision[s] sufficient to have lasted us several months in California," Virginia noted.

The Reeds and Donners consulted their guidebook before packing. Here are the approximate amounts of food, per adult, brought along for daily meals:

> 200 pounds of flour
> 150 pounds of bacon
> 20 pounds of sugar
> 10 pounds of coffee
> 10 pounds of salt
> Various amounts of cornmeal, cured or "jerked" meats, dried beans, fruit, tea, baking soda, vinegar, pickles, and mustard

Aside from a few trading posts along the way, there would be no place to shop.

The families carried trinkets for the Native Americans, hoping to head off trouble by offering small gifts of coins and jewels. They also brought silks, laces, and gold pieces, in case they had to bargain with the Mexicans. Tamsen Donner, George's well-educated wife, packed textbooks and watercolors. Tamsen, who had taught school in her home state of Massachusetts and in North Carolina, planned to open a "young ladies' seminary" in California.

It was also rumored that the Donners had a quilt with ten thousand dollars in cash sewn inside. James Reed had gold pieces, a letter of reference signed by the governor of Illinois, and a medal signifying his membership in the Masons, a fraternal organization.

Everyone had new clothes, sewn especially for the journey. The girls' outfits were quite a change for them, as Virginia noted:

> Our clothing was made suitable for trav[e]ling, dresses of plaid linsy [linen], aprons of Scotch ging[h]am, high in the neck, with long sleeves, belt waists and little collars. No more use for low necked, short sleeved, pretty little white dresses, with blue and pink sashes, and cute little slippers. All those things were givin away. I remember when I first dressed up in my uniform for the planes [plains], as we called it, How strangely I felt. The very clothing seemed to indicate that we were expected to endure something.

The nine wagons finally lined up. George and Tamsen Donner and their five daughters assembled. Jacob Donner and his wife, Elizabeth, gathered up their brood of seven. The Pioneer Palace Car held Virginia's mother and siblings: eight-year-old Martha (nicknamed Patty, or Matty), five-year-old James Jr., and three-year-old Thomas.

Virginia's uncles carried Grandma Keyes to the wagon and laid her gently in her feather bed, "as tenderly and carefully as a loved one is placed in a coffin." Sarah Keyes knew her days were numbered, but her youngest son had emigrated west the previous year and she hoped to see him again before she died. "My little, black-eyed sister Patty sat on the bed and held up the wagon cover so Grandma might have a last look at her old home," Virginia said.

The company also included several young single men who had answered

Patty Reed

(California State Parks, Sutter's Fort State Historical Park)

George Donner's ad. They would do the hard physical labor. These teamsters, as they were called, brought the Springfield group to a total of thirty-two.

The teamsters took their places, standing beside the teams of oxen that were yoked to the tongues of the wagons. With baggage this heavy, the men didn't drive the oxen by sitting behind them but by walking beside them and whipping them along. In effect, the teamsters would be traveling the twenty-five hundred miles from Illinois to California on foot.

At the end of the wagon train were a few horses, spare oxen, and cows to provide milk. The families brought their dogs along, too. The Reeds had five: Barney, Tyler, Tracker, Trailer, and the little terrier, Cash, the children's pet.

James Reed took the lead on his new mare, Glaucus. Being a fine race-horse, not a plodding plow animal, she drew stares. So, probably, did the biggest oxen—the ones pulling the Pioneer Palace Car. No doubt Reed enjoyed many murmurs of admiration. Legend has it that Mary Todd Lincoln was among the neighbors who pressed forward to say good-bye and to bring

Mary Todd Lincoln
(*Library of Congress*)

good wishes from her husband, Abe, who was away at circuit court.

Virginia came alongside on Billy, proud to be riding to California under her own power. Seeing her next to James Reed, it would be hard to believe she was actually his stepdaughter. Her real father had died when Virginia was a baby. To the world, and in Virginia's heart, James Reed was her father. She never referred to him in any other way.

When Virginia saw her mother sobbing, she wasn't surprised. "My mothe[r] who had kept up so bravely was now over come with greafe and had to be almost carried out of the house also."

But her father?

[H]e went through dashing the teares from his eyes shaking hands right and left with every body. And last but not least were all my little school mates, girles and boys who had come to bid me good-by. Uncles & Aunts, Cousins & friends were all to be left. I have neve[r] liked to say the word "good-by" to any one since that day. . . .

All wished us good luck & [teamster] Milt Elliot our Knight of the ox whip cryed 'all aboard for California' and so we left our old home . . . full of hope and corage.

Indeed, if I do not experience something far worse than I have done,
I shall say the trouble is all in getting started.

—Tamsen Donner, in a letter to her sister, June 1846

ᏺᎻᎻᎯ

CHAPTER 2

Independence and Beyond

The first big landmark for the Reeds and Donners was Independence, Missouri, almost three hundred miles west of Springfield. This city was the crossroads for pioneers heading west to California or Oregon or south along the Santa Fe Trail. It would be an easy journey of three weeks to one month; the wagon train could cover up to fifteen miles a day at a fast walking pace, if all went well. No reason it shouldn't: The well-used trail was so carved by deep ruts that the wagons might have rolled there themselves.

And things were going well. Relatives and friends of the Donners and Reeds "came & camped with us on the first night," Virginia recalled. "Uncle Gersham came with us several days. Finally all had gone back, and we began to realize that we were really on our journey." The days took on a slow but steady rhythm, like the progress of the wagon train itself.

The families set up camp each night by the Missouri River or its feeder streams. In these waters, or from well-marked springs along the way, they led the cattle to drink and drew water for drinking and washing.

On some wagon trains, women and children helped to drive the oxen. The Donners and Reeds, however, employed young men to do the work. *(Library of Congress)*

Everyone over age five did chores. Women's work included cooking, mending, laundering, and child tending, although children over seven were considered to have reached "the age of reason" and not in need of constant supervision. The men tended the animals, drove the oxen, maintained the wagons, and hunted. They were not expert hunters, having worked on farms most of their lives. Wringing chickens' necks and butchering livestock does not prepare a person to target a fast-moving antelope or deer.

Roles did overlap sometimes. Virginia could help handle the horses, if needed, and fathers were not above holding washed diapers over the campfire to dry. Everyone chipped in to gather berries and catch fish.

Mornings, Virginia helped the women prepare breakfasts of cornmeal mush or hominy grits, salt pork or bacon. Bread was baked in the coals of the campfire the night before, in the big covered pots called Dutch ovens, or in skillets over the fire. Lunch didn't require cooking; it was usually more bread and beef jerky. Every meal included dried fruit, eaten to ward off scurvy, an

A reproduction of a typical kitchen wagon. Like a cabinet, it stored dishes, jugs, coffee grinders, butter churns, and other items. Flour, dried fruit, and other daily food supplies were stored in sacks at the other end. *(Marian Calabro)*

illness that made the gums bleed. Grilled meat or fish was the main course at dinner.

The families ate sitting on the ground, on ponchos made of India rubber. It was the girls' job to take the utensils and plates from their cloth bags—they got dusty right away if kept out—and to scrub everything after meals with gritty dirt or sand before rinsing and repacking.

Food couldn't be kept cold, but the travelers had butter, churned from the cows' fresh milk. "Some times it would almost be Churned from the jolting," Virginia wrote.

During the long mornings and afternoons, the women and girls knitted, quilted, read, exchanged recipes, and chatted as they rode along. The caravan moved so slowly that people could easily jump on and off the wagons to visit. Virginia did less of this because she was usually outside:

Most of my time was spent on horseback with my father. My Mother would come with us some times, but she prefered the comfortable wagon   did not feel like raceing ove[r] the country as I did . . . we would mount our horses, ride along with the wagons for a while. and then start of[f] to have a nearer vew of something we saw in the distance, but were always on hand for lunch. I gathered many wild flowers and brought to camp   some of them were beautiful. after lunch we often raced ahead and picked out a good camping ground.

Evenings were mellow. The families would circle the wagons to keep out the wind and dig holes in the ground for their individual cooking fires. After eating supper and cleaning up, everyone relaxed around a communal bonfire. The kids played ball and tag and threw sticks for the dogs to retrieve, until it got too dark to see.

As night fell, they would, in Virginia's words, "gather about the camp fire, chatting merrily, and often a song would be heard, or some clever dancer would give us a barn-door jig on the hind gate of a wagon." No doubt they sang songs from all the places they had lived: ballads of Appalachia, like the mournful "Shenandoah" and "The Cumberland Gap"; silly tunes like "My Sweetheart's a Mule"; and sea chanties from coastal Massachusetts, where Tamsen Donner grew up. An old British song that James Reed almost certainly would have heard on his boyhood voyage from Ireland to America was a favorite in those days, as it is with folk singers today:

> There was a lofty ship, and she put out to sea,
> And she goes by the name of the Golden Vanity,
> And we feared she would be taken by the Spanish enemy,
> As we sailed along the lowland, lonesome, low,
> As we sailed along the lowland sea.

"The Golden Vanity" goes on for many verses, the tale of a young sailor who bravely sank the enemy ship, then was left to drown by his own fickle captain. How much safer to be on land, Virginia might have mused; oceans, like mountains, were another thing she hadn't seen yet.

Each day, life in Springfield slipped farther away. Back there the days would have been routine. This adventure, while it had its own routines, was better. "I know I was perfectly happy," Virginia said later, remembering the first golden days.

꘎

Westbound wagon trains faced several kinds of danger: bad weather, illness, deserts, mountains, and Indians.

The idea of Indians began to loom in Virginia's mind as the pioneers came into open territory. Grandma Keyes, who had emigrated to Illinois from her home state of Virginia, often talked about an aunt who had been held hostage for five years by a tribe there. Whether or not the story was true, it made a strong impression on Virginia:

> I was always begging her to tell me about her Aunt, sometimes I would be frightened, would be afraid to look behind me, felt sure [an Indian] would be standing behind me with raised Tommahawk over my head, and then I would go and sit with my back up against the wall and beg her to go on.

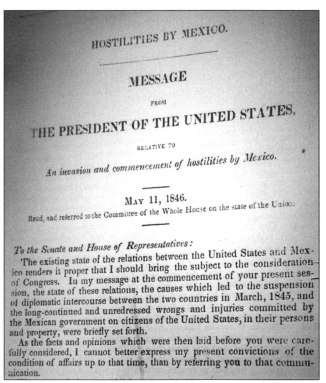

War with Mexico posed unknown dangers for westbound wagon trains. President James K. Polk issued this warning just as the Reeds and Donners were about to leave Missouri, which (with Texas) was then the westernmost state. *(Marian Calabro. Photographed at Sutter's Fort State Historical Park)*

However, the first trouble was far duller than a tomahawk attack. It rained for days. The foul weather brought home the drawbacks of not living in a real house.

While spring showers were common, May 1846 brought thunderous storms. The westbound trail, already deeply rutted, became a sea of mud. Wagons spun their wheels and were mired to the hubs. The more the oxen strained, the deeper the wagons sank. The teamsters strained to push them out and get the caravan moving again.

The canvas walls and roofs of the wagons soaked up the rains and swelled. To touch them from inside was to invite a leak—irresistible fun for the little ones, maddening to parents and older sisters trying to keep supplies dry. Those pleasant outdoor evenings gave way to hasty cooking under tents. Clothes couldn't be dried very well, diapers included, and neither could bodies.

Drenched and mud-splattered, the Reeds and Donners reached Independence, Missouri, in twenty-five days, on May 11. At twelve miles a day that pace was slower than planned, but they hoped to make up for lost time.

Independence was crowded. Emigrants were buying supplies, trading advice about routes, and rushing on. An evangelist stopped at each wagon, giving each child his or her own Bible.

"I can give you no idea of the hurry of this place at this time," Tamsen Donner wrote to her sister in Newburyport, Massachusetts. "It is supposed there will be 7000 waggons will start from this place this season. We go to California, to the bay of San Francisco. It is a four months trip. I am willing to go & have no doubt it will be an advantage to our children & to us."

The Reed women were less enthusiastic. "Margrat [Margaret] and your mother were in low spirits yesterd[a]y, when they wondered that this [journey] won't be someday regretted," James Reed wrote to his brother-in-law in Springfield.

༺⚊⚊༻

Independence was "the jumping-off spot," the place where pioneers jumped off into the untamed land beyond the established United States. Probably it was where Margaret Reed had to face the fact that the Reeds would not turn back.

For safety, the Reeds and Donners began to travel with a bigger wagon

Independence, Missouri, a few years after the Reeds and Donners passed through *(Kansas State Historical Society)*

train, captained by William Russell. This was for two reasons—they expected to encounter Native Americans, and a war was heating up. The war was between Mexico, which claimed California, and the United States, which wanted it.

But war seemed far away. When the rains stopped the trip resumed a more relaxed feeling. Summer was coming; the air smelled grainy and sweet as the families crossed Kansas. The prairie was lush with green grass and wildflowers. Virginia happily spent whole days on her pony. "The younger [women] and the girls passed [their time] in the saddle," recalled Eliza Donner, Tamsen's daughter. "The wild, free spirit of the plain often prompted them to invite us little ones to seats behind them, and away we would canter with the breeze playing through our hair."

Virginia felt sadness as well, when her grandmother died on May 29, near modern-day Alcove Springs, Kansas. Sarah Keyes had been suffering for a year with consumption, the vague name in those days for diseases (especially tuberculosis) that "consumed" a person's body. As she slipped away, she lost her sight and appetite. Sarah's dream of seeing her son would not be fulfilled. "My poor mothe[r] was almost heartbroken," Virginia said, and "my little sister who had nursed [Grandma] all the way—stayed in the wagon with her all the time, was inconsolable."

Virginia wrote to her cousins in Illinois with the news. Although her spelling was shaky, her feelings were clear:

> Gramma died, she became spechless the day before she died. We buried her verry decent We made a nete coffin and buried her under a tree We had a head stone and had her name cut on it and the date and yere verry nice. . . . We miss her verry much every time we come into the Wagon we look at the bed for her.

In June, the company crossed flat, dusty Nebraska territory. After an unseasonably chilly week, the weather grew so hot that the sun baked the inside of the wagons to well above one hundred degrees Fahrenheit by mid-morning. People took turns riding horses, or they walked, wearing hats with big brims. As they moved into the treeless plains, it became a game to collect buffalo dung, called chips, which took the place of wood to start the evening fires.

Virginia was more interested in hunting the buffalo themselves:

> I was very anxious to go with my father hunting Buffalo but he knew it was dangerous and would not take me. One evening, howeve[r] as we were coming in to camp, we came across a small herd and started after them. They broke for the camp. Of course we were frightened, but could not head them off. Just before they reached thare they shied and passed on. When I saw no one was hurt I could [not] help laughing to see the way the wemen and children were jumping into the wagons knocking over every thing around the Camp. My Mothe[r] said *that* was some of my work and that my fathe[r] was spoiling me.

Buffalo (a species of bison) blanketed the plains. James Reed hunted them avidly, partly for food and partly to show off. He wanted to be seen as "the best and most daring horseman in the caravan." After one hunt, in which he counted 597 buffalo and shot two, Reed boasted that he was "the acknowledged hero of the day and the most successful buffalo hunter on the route." *(Library of Congress)*

Generally, James Reed and the other buffalo hunters were successful. Buffalo steaks became a regular item for dinner. "The meat of a young Buffalo is excelent," Virginia said.

At the army post of Fort Kearney, they reached the Platte River. "Moving sand," some emigrants called it. But the slow river was a reliable route from Nebraska into Wyoming. (Today, Interstate 80 parallels it from Omaha to Cheyenne.) Sometimes the terrain forced them to cross and recross the Platte, which took time. The men had to swim the cattle across, then regrease and often reset the wagon wheels afterward. If the water was high, the women had to unpack the goods from the wagons and raft them across—then reload them on the other side.

Still, the sluggish Platte River led the families past all the natural land-

An unknown wagon train crosses the Platte River. This type of crossing was relatively easy. If the water had been higher, the wagons would have been detached from their wheels and floated across on rafts. *(Nebraska State Historical Society)*

marks they had read about in *The Emigrants' Guide to Oregon and California*, including Courthouse Rock, Chimney Rock, and Scotts Bluff. "I never could have believed we could have traveled so far with so little difficulty," Tamsen Donner wrote to her sister in June.

"I wrote my fathe[r's] name on Chimney Rock and every other place that I could," Virginia said. "I used to amuse myself in that way."

Virginia Reed turned thirteen on June 28. There is no record of any celebration, but we do know that hints of trouble arose around that date. Near the first landmark in eastern Wyoming territory, the fur-trading outpost of Fort Laramie, the families met some frontiersmen returning from California. One was James Clyman, a well-known Western explorer. Clyman clearly warned the travelers to avoid the shortcut recommended by Lansford Hastings, author of the guidebook the Donners and Reeds were following.

"I told Reed to take the regular wagon track and never leave it—it is barely possible to get through if you follow it—and maybe impossible if you don't," Clyman said. "I told him about the great desert and the roughness of the Sierra, and that a straight route might turn out to be impracticable," especially for covered wagons.

Reed brushed off the warnings. It is hard to say why, especially because Clyman was not a stranger; he had served with Reed and Abraham Lincoln in the Black Hawk War. Perhaps Reed leaned toward Hastings because he was a self-made professional man, like Reed himself. No doubt he admired the fact that Hastings had published a *book* on the subject, while Clyman was a rough-and-ready mountain man. What really swayed Reed, however, was the idea of cutting the long journey by 350 to 400 miles.

Besides, things were going smoothly. Most wagon trains reached Independence Rock—a huge boulder marking the start of the Rocky Mountains, where emigrants inscribed their names—by Independence Day. The Reeds and Donners were about a week late, but making steady progress.

Independence Rock in Wyoming. Soon the emigrants would begin climbing the Rocky Mountains. (*Wyoming Division of Cultural Resources*)

This Fourth of July, America was turning seventy years old. Chores and fears were put aside; fun came first on a holiday, as Virginia described in a letter to her cousin:

Severel of the gentlemen in Springfield gave paw a botel of licker and said it shoulden be opend til the 4 day of July and paw was to look to the east & drink it & thay was to look to the west & drink it at 12 o'clock paw treted the company and we [children] all had some lemminade.

At last they came to that danger Virginia had dreaded: Indians on the warpath. In Kansas the emigrants had been ferried across the Caw River (now called the Kansas River) by members of the Caw tribe. Much to Virginia's surprise, those Native Americans had been peaceful: "Oh! but I was

A Sioux war party. Virginia wrote with excitement to her cousins in Illinois that the Sioux were "going to war with the crow . . . we have to pass throw ther fiting ground . . . the Soux Indians are the pretest drest [prettiest dressed] Indians thare is." *(Library of Congress)*

frightened. I was sure they would drown us and told my fathe[r] so. . . . I would not let them get behind me." But the businesslike Caw "were not like Grandma's Indians." In Wyoming territory, however, some Sioux were pursuing enemy bands of Blackfoot and Crow. They looked frightening in their war costumes, sporting huge feather headdresses. Yet, as Virginia found, there was little to fear:

> Some of our company became alarmed, and the rifles were cleaned out and loaded, to let the warriors see that we were prepared to fight; but the Sioux never showed any inclination to disturb us. . . . but our wagon with its conspicuous stove pipe and looking glass attracted their attention. They were continuously swarming about trying to get a look at themselves in the mirror . . . as I pulled it out with a click, the warriors jumped back, wheeled their ponies and scattered. This pleased me greatly, and I told my mother I could fight the whole Sioux tribe with a spyglass . . . whenever they came near trying to get a peep at their war-paint and feathers, I would raise the glass and laugh to see them dart away in terror.

In fact, she noted, the Sioux "fell in love with my pony and set about bargaining to buy him." Apparently they had never seen this breed of horse. They offered brass buttons, precious buffalo robes, and several of their own valuable horses, making "large offers for him." Of course, Billy was not for sale.

Virginia "was awfully provoked for I had to ride in the wagon while they were around. My fathe[r] was afraid they would steal the pony and had some of the men ride him . . . until they were all gone, and then Billy and I were free again, bounding over the plains almost as wild as the Indians."

Like most whites of the time, the group felt superior to Native Americans. However, they tried to keep up good relations for the sake of barter, sometimes trading calico cloth or coins for salmon or buffalo. Many pioneer men found that the women were better at these dealings and often let them handle the negotiations.

Throughout the summer, as the group crossed Nebraska and Wyoming, the wagon train grew.

In Virginia's eyes, the best addition to the Reed-Donner Party was probably the Breen family. Patrick and Peggy Breen, Irish-born but from Iowa, had just become U.S. citizens. They were farmers, had six boys and a baby girl, and could read and write, unlike many emigrants of the 1840s. Their oldest sons, John and Edward, became friends with Virginia and Patty. Patrick Breen played the violin, adding music to the bonfire gatherings at night.

And everyone enjoyed being around Patrick Dolan, a young bachelor friend of the Breens who traveled in his own wagon. Dolan was musical, too, always ready to sing or do the Irish jig.

Margaret and Patrick Breen (with beard) and their oldest son, John *(California State Parks, Sutter's Fort State Historical Park)*

The William Eddy family from Illinois—a young man, his wife, and their two babies—was another welcome addition. A professional carriage maker, William could do much-needed repairs on the wagons. He was also a good hunter and generous about sharing his catch.

Also new was Levinah Murphy's clan, from Tennessee and Illinois, the only family in the group to be headed by a woman. Thirty-six-year-old Levinah had been widowed seven years earlier with seven children. Her two oldest daughters, still teenagers, were married. They were along with their own young families, the Pikes and the Fosters.

Having grown up on her family's South Carolina plantation, Levinah Murphy was at least as well born as the families from Springfield. But circumstances had forced her to be independent, and she might have appeared tougher than the Donner and Reed women, who were also widowed but had remarried. Levinah may also have stood out for another reason — as a recent Mormon convert, she may have been moving west for religious freedom as well as land.

Maybe it was the age-old distrust of outsiders, or maybe personalities just didn't mesh, but the Murphy clan and the Reeds and Donners always seemed wary of one another. Social differences probably accounted for some of the coolness.

A small group of German-born travelers, including the Kesebergs and Wolfingers, also joined the company. They had emigrated to the United States a few years earlier and seemed well off. Louis Keseberg spoke three languages, and Mrs. Wolfinger wore showy jewelry. For these reasons, perhaps, the Springfielders felt a little uneasy with them. Also, Keseberg beat his wife, which James Reed in particular could not tolerate.

In a wagon train or party that had joined forces for practical reasons, people couldn't ignore one another. They had to communicate and work together at certain tasks. Nonetheless, the original Springfield families and the newcomers kept a certain psychological distance from each other. Traveling together was basically a business arrangement.

Tamsen Donner described the situation this way: "We have some of the best people in our company and some, too, that are not so good." However, as long as everyone remained civil and tensions stayed small, no one worried too much. The point for all of them was not to be best friends but to move ahead to California.

My father was so eager to reach California that he was quick to take advantage of any means to shorten the distance. . . . a few days showed us that the [shortcut] was not as it had been represented. . . . There was absolutely no road, not even a trail.

—Virginia Reed

ᠸᠠᠠᠥ

CHAPTER 3

Shortcut to Danger

James Reed and the Donner brothers were independent-minded men, but they were under the influence of *The Emigrants' Guide to Oregon and California*. They had bought this book in Springfield and taken it along to consult on the trail.

It offered more propaganda than guidance: thirteen chapters of the author's own experiences and musings on the wonders of the West, but only two chapters of how-to travel advice. Buried within was brief mention of a shortcut:

> The most direct route, for the California emigrants, would be to leave the Oregon route, about two hundred miles east from Fort Hall; then bearing west southwest, to the Salt Lake; and thence continuing down to the bay of San Francisco.

The only trouble was that the guide's author, Lansford Warren Hastings, had not done this route himself with a wagon train. No one had.

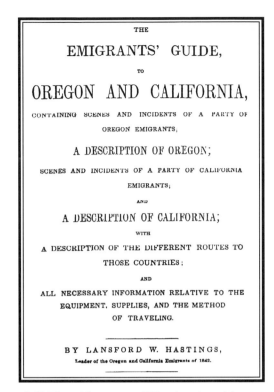

(left) The title page of Hastings's guide *(Author's collection)* *(right)* Lansford Warren Hastings *(Library of Congress)*

Hastings, a lawyer, was part visionary and part fraud. He had delusions of greatness. Born and raised in Ohio, he somehow decided he was meant to be the president or emperor of California, which he first visited in 1843. Hastings felt he could win California from Mexico and establish it as an independent nation.

Hastings's inspiration might have been Sam Houston, president of the Republic of Texas from 1836 to 1838 and 1841 to 1844. But Hastings sorely lacked Sam Houston's leadership experience. Mainly he wanted followers, preferably white settlers, to populate his would-be empire. So he returned to the United States to promote his book and to lecture about the lure of California, praising its ideal climate and untold riches. To steer people away from Oregon, which was more populated, he cleverly made it sound less enticing than California. Clearly, Hastings had magnetism; one observer called him "handsome, strong-faced, quick and intelligent of speech."

To be fair, Lansford Hastings was not the first person to believe there was a shorter route to California—one that didn't zigzag north to avoid the Great Salt Lake Desert but went straight west from the Rocky Mountains to the Sierra Nevada of California. The earliest white explorers, John C. Frémont and Jedediah Smith, searched for the Buenaventura, a miraculous stream said to cut through the towering, treacherous sierra, the mountain chain that rises like a wall between California and the rest of the United States. But Frémont and Smith made their first explorations some twenty years before the Donner Party, and even they had not discovered the Buenaventura in the meantime, because it was not there to be found.

And certainly Reed and the Donners were not the only ones who took Hastings seriously. The man and his book inspired hundreds of emigrants, perhaps thousands, to head west. However, the shortcut that the guidebook mentioned—called the Hastings Cutoff—came more than halfway into the established route. By then, most travelers were content to take the longer, safer, proven trail via Fort Hall to California.

John Charles Frémont, an early explorer of the West *(Library of Congress)*

For the Donner Party, the decision point came on a hot summer day, July 20. They crossed the summit of the Rocky Mountains—over a long, easy pass in what is modern-day southwest Wyoming—and descended to the Sandy River. A right turn here was the fastest way to Fort Hall. Straight on, Hastings's route took them to Fort Bridger, the Great Salt Lake, and the desert beyond. While his shortcut was untested by travelers with wagons, it promised to save up to four hundred precious miles.

By now, the Donner Party knew they moved slowly. Their twenty-two wagons lumbered along, and they tended to dawdle: one rest day here, two rest days there. They covered an average of eleven miles a day, not the fifteen to twenty they'd planned. After three months, they were barely halfway to

The parting of the ways. The main road led to Fort Hall. The left fork led to Fort Bridger and the Hastings Cutoff. (*Wyoming Division of Cultural Resources*)

California. Much of the Russell Party, with whom they had been traveling, was now well ahead of them.

James Reed continued to argue that the Hastings Cutoff would save them a month and get them over the Sierra Nevada by September, well before the heavy snows began.

Some of the group, especially the women, continued to doubt the unknown shortcut.

Virginia's father played his winning card: an "open letter" from Hastings himself, delivered about a week earlier by a passing traveler. The guidebook author, who was leading other emigrants to California, was ahead of the Donner Party by a few days. In his letter, Hastings promised to backtrack toward Fort Bridger and personally escort the rest of the travelers through the shortcut. What more assurance, James Reed must have asked, could anyone want?

Finally, the group took a vote, which was standard practice in wagon trains.

If the women had been allowed to cast ballots, the results might have been different. But women didn't yet have the right to vote in general society, much less on the trail. The majority of men—as well as the boys over the age of fourteen, who were regarded as adults and thus permitted to vote—sided with James Reed. (One refused to accept the vote, however. Hiram Miller, a Donner teamster and bachelor who had been along since Springfield, left the group to travel by way of Fort Hall.)

The divided feelings were evident to one observer. In the words of Jessy Quinn Thornton, an 1846 pioneer who later wrote about his travels, Reed and his followers were:

Much elated and in fine spirits, with the prospect of a better and nearer road to the country of their destination. Mrs. George Donner was, however, an exception. She was gloomy, sad, and dispirited in view of the fact that her husband and others could think for a moment of leaving the old road, and confide in the statement of a man of whom they knew nothing, but who was probably some selfish adventurer.

It seems that Tamsen Donner and Hiram Miller were not the only people who lacked full faith in James Reed. The group took a vote on another essential decision.

They chose an official captain: amiable George Donner, known by all as Uncle George. The emigrants under his leadership would now and forever be known as the Donner Party.

If James Reed felt slighted, he could console himself that George Donner had won only a battle, while he, Reed, had won a war.

༺༻

In retrospect, viewed charitably, Lansford Hastings had some scruples—perhaps. Knowing that the directions in his book were vague, he had set out early in 1846 to field-test his shortcut. He took along two of the most famous mountain men in the West, James Clyman and Caleb Greenwood.

These two skilled explorers found Hastings's route almost impossible. The

James Clyman knew the dangers of the road that the Donner Party was about to take. He had been exploring and trapping in the West for more than twenty years. *(Library of Congress)*

salt deserts were brutal to cross; there was no water to be had for days. The Wasatch mountain range, thickly forested and dotted with steep canyons, was hard to navigate on foot and horseback. To traverse it in large, ox-drawn wagons would be suicide. James Clyman was so outraged that he took it upon himself to head back along the main trail, determined to warn every advancing wagon train against the Hastings Cutoff. Clyman was the one who had caught up with the Donners and Reeds and issued his anti-Hastings warning back near Fort Laramie, three weeks before they took their vote.

James Reed's reply to Clyman has come down through history. It resounds with the sincerity of his belief in Hastings and the depths of his own ignorance about the West: "There is a nearer route, and it is of no use to take so much of a roundabout course."

ᏬᎱᎳᎲ

Virginia adored her father and echoed his belief in their plans. "Without suspicion of impending disaster, we set out with high spirits on the Hastings Cut-off," she said. The date was July 31, and the weather was still hot.

Hastings wasn't waiting at Fort Bridger, as he had promised. He was leading two other groups, a big train of more than sixty wagons. The Donner Party would follow their tracks and meet up with Hastings soon enough, by James Reed's reckoning.

Because Fort Bridger was the last place to stock up on supplies before California, they stayed there briefly—long enough to make repairs to their equipment, buy new livestock, wash their clothes, and cram the wagons full of flour, sugar, and dried beef. Each day they were assured by the fort's proprietor, the noted western explorer James Bridger, that taking the Hastings Cutoff was absolutely the right thing to do.

Bridger was lying. He promoted the shortcut because he desperately needed the business it could bring. Emigrants had been bypassing his trading post since a branch road to Fort Hall, known as Caleb Greenwood's Cutoff, had been blazed two years earlier. Also, Lansford Hastings may have paid Bridger and his partner, Louis Vasquez, to tout his route.

In fact, Vasquez had conveniently failed to deliver letters of warning to James Reed from Edwin Bryant, a friend who had traveled with the Donners

(above) Fort Bridger, a trading post, was off the main route. Proprietors James Bridger and Louis Vasquez charged high prices, but the Donner Party had to pay. The next place to stock up on supplies was more than six hundred miles away.
(Wyoming Division of Cultural Resources)

(right)
James Bridger
(Library of Congress)

and Reeds part of the way but was now far ahead. Bryant sent back several letters urging Reed and everyone else not to take the cutoff. He had just done it with a few other men traveling solo, on mules, and found it almost impossible.

"We could afford to hazard experiments, and make explorations," Bryant wrote. "They [those with wagons and families] could not."

But James Reed never received those warnings. And he had no reason to suspect Bridger's honesty. Reed expected a bad patch along the shortcut, an estimated "40 miles without water." The remainder of the route, he believed, would be easy. In this letter to relatives in Springfield, Reed's air of confidence shines through:

On the new route we will not have dust, as there are about 60 waggons ahead of us. . . . The rest of the [California-bound emigrants] went the long route feeling afraid of Hastings Cutoff. Mr. Bridger informs me that the route we design to take, is a fine level road, with plenty of water and grass, with the exception before stated [40 miles without water]. . . . It is estimated that 700 miles will take us to Capt. Sutter's Fort, which we hope to make in seven weeks from this day.

*

As a smart and cautious person, Tamsen Donner must have agonized over the fact that Fort Bridger was the last chance to return to the main route. A few days of backtracking would bring them to Fort Hall. They wouldn't be far behind the hundreds of other emigrants, like Hiram Miller, who had gone that way. But their course was set now. And almost immediately they had the kind of accident that Tamsen and the other mothers had dreaded all along the way.

So far the Donner Party had escaped the possible misfortunes of emigrant trains—sudden and disabling illness, someone falling from a moving wagon, or a small child getting lost in the crowded confusion of Independence or Fort Kearney. Their good luck was tested just west of Fort Bridger.

Edward Breen, thirteen, had become friends with both Reed girls, especially Patty. He and Patty were galloping side by side on horseback when

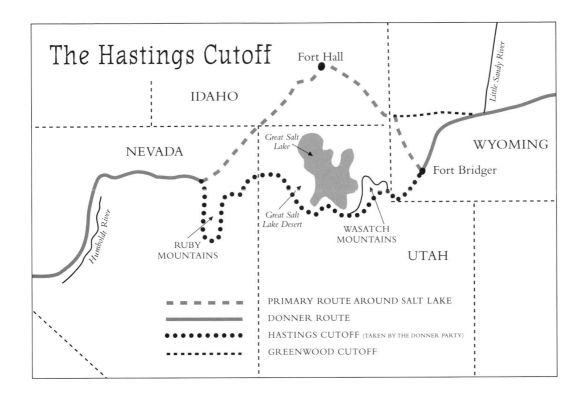

The Hastings Cutoff

Fort Hall

IDAHO

Little Sandy River

Great Salt Lake

WYOMING

Fort Bridger

NEVADA

Great Salt Lake Desert

Humboldt River

RUBY MOUNTAINS

WASATCH MOUNTAINS

UTAH

PRIMARY ROUTE AROUND SALT LAKE
DONNER ROUTE
HASTINGS CUTOFF (TAKEN BY THE DONNER PARTY)
GREENWOOD CUTOFF

Edward's pony "put one or both front feet into a badger or prairie dog burrow and took a hard fall."

Edward landed hard and was knocked unconscious. It was evident to Patty, and to the others who clustered around them, that his left leg was badly broken between the knee and ankle.

Edward lived to tell and retell the rest of the story, which became a Breen family legend and is repeated here in the words of his son:

Someone was sent back to the Fort for aid in repairing the damage, and after what seemed a long time, a rough-looking man with long whiskers rode up on a mule. He examined [Edward's] leg and proceeded to unroll a small bundle he had wrapped in canvas and tied behind his saddle. Out of this came a short meat saw and a long bladed knife.

Amputation of a limb was a not-uncommon "remedy" in those days. But Edward was now awake and protesting. "The boy set up a loud cry when he

Edward Breen as an adult. His broken leg came at an especially bad time. The Donner Party was already short on people strong enough to cut a route through the thickly forested Wasatch Mountains. *(California State Library)*

sensed what was to be done and finally after a long discussion convinced his parents that he should keep his leg. The old mountain man was given five dollars and sent back to the Fort, muttering to himself for not being given a chance to display his skill as a "surgeon."

Patty and Virginia lost a riding partner, but they could keep Edward company in his family's wagon while he lay with his leg splinted with wooden boards. The teenager healed fast; he was back on his horse eight weeks later. But so much happened in between that Edward's accident seemed harmless by comparison.

Within a few days they knew Hastings Cutoff was a fraud. There was no road, no trail, only the barest path through wilderness.

Most maddening of all, there was no Lansford Hastings.

Some of the hills were so steep that the wagons threatened to somersault. Then the Donner Party would lock the wagon wheels, slide straight downhill, and pray. Other times they would have to yoke all the oxen to one wagon, pull it uphill, and return for the next; or they used chains and pulleys to winch themselves upward. Some of the land was so rocky that the clatter of their wheels resounded for miles. And they wondered if Indians, hostile ones, were listening and watching.

On August 6, they found a note on a stick. Hastings wrote that because he was so busy leading the other parties, he couldn't turn back just yet. But he wanted the Donner Party to know that the trail ahead was very bad. They should wait for him to return and show them a better route.

Even the tiniest children knew that the area they had reached was impassable. They were at the top of Weber Canyon, which James Reed described in his diary as "walls narrowed to precipices on either side of a river." The party

Weber Canyon in 1869, after the creation of the Union Pacific Railroad. Unable to cross this treacherous stretch with wagons, the Donner Party had to scout a long route around it. *(Union Pacific Museum Collection)*

literally could not move ahead without plunging off cliffs. To move the wagons they would have to take them apart, lower the pieces over the cliffs, then reassemble the vehicles and repeat the process who knew how many times. Getting the people down seemed totally impossible.

All eyes turned to Reed, Hastings's champion.

Reed prided himself on being a man of action. Swearing to catch up with Hastings and demand some answers, he left on horseback with William Pike and Charles Stanton, an energetic bachelor in his thirties. In other terrain, the trio would have galloped off in clouds of dust. Instead, they had to painstakingly pick their way down the canyon walls.

The others set up camp and waited. Waited. Waited.

❦

Reed caught up with Hastings—it was their first actual meeting—but Hastings refused to return. He had his obligations to the groups he was leading, after all; they themselves had suffered through crossing Weber Canyon and were not in the best shape. But, of course Hastings could suggest an alternate route. He camped with Reed one night and pointed it out from a mountaintop. Did Hastings really know this route? Even James Reed didn't trust him now.

Stanton and Pike rested at Hastings's camp, because their horses had been taxed almost to death. So had Reed's horse, but Reed forced Hastings to give him another. Then Reed blazed his own trail back, traveling alone and marking the trees as he went. He got back to the Donner Party, and they followed Reed's route away from Weber Canyon.

Weren't Stanton and Pike coming back? No one knew, and there was no time to wait or look for them.

❦

One week was lost while camped at Weber Canyon. Then the party moved in excruciatingly slow motion. Days were spent pulleying the wagons down canyons by rope and tackle, chopping down trees one ax stroke at a time. The hands of the men were swollen with painful blisters from all the ax work; their shoulders never stopped aching. The Donner Party was hacking out its own route, known today as Emigration Canyon. They cleared a path through canyons dense with willow, aspen, and cottonwood trees, day after torturous day with no seeming end.

Clawing their way through the Wasatch Mountains, they faced some of the toughest terrain in the West. And the mountain man who hadn't written a book, James Clyman, had warned them all about it.

Clearing a trail through the Wasatch was work for strong young men, who were in the minority in the Donner Party. Miraculously, on the third day in the Wasatch, some new travelers joined them. Franklin Graves and his extended family, emigrant farmers from Illinois, traveled even more slowly than the Donner group. After following in their tracks for days, they had finally caught

In his diary, James Reed recorded the agonizingly slow progress through the Wasatch Mountains of Utah. Monday, August 17: "Still in camp and all hands working on the road. . . ." Thursday, August 20: "Still in camp and hands clearing road."

The last three entries end with each day's mileage—4, 2, 5—a far cry from the fifteen miles a day the Donner Party hoped to do on the "shortcut." (*Author's collection*)

up. They brought the group to its full strength: eighty-seven people in twenty-three wagons. Best of all, among the thirteen Graves family members were four young men who had sufficient energy to help clear the trail.

Then came more luck. Stanton and Pike reappeared. They were so starved they were about to kill and eat their horses. After leaving Hastings's camp, they had gotten lost; as a result, they had covered a fair part of this territory. So they could help scout the way out.

Still, the Donner Party was barely advancing two miles a day. Some days were spent cutting through thickets of thorn bushes that slapped them in the face. Some mornings they spent hours rolling a single boulder from a narrow creek bed in order to go forward. Energy plummeted. Food supplies dwindled. Anger simmered.

The feeling in the group was hardly cooperative. William Graves, son of Franklin, said of James Reed: "Reed, being an aristocratic fellow, was above working, so he had hired hands to drive his teams and he gave orders, although no one paid much attention to him; but his wife was a lady and the company humored him a good deal on that account."

Virginia Reed said, "Finally we reached the end of the Canyon. Worn with travel and greatly discouraged, we reached the shore of the Great [Salt] Lake."

Like her father, like everyone, Virginia had a keen sense of what Hastings's empty promises had cost them. So far the shortcut "had taken us an entire month, instead of a week, and our cattle were not fit to cross the desert."

And, at some point, Virginia lost her pony. No history of the Donner Party says exactly where. But in recollections made years later, Virginia's pain still seemed fresh:

Every morning I would stroke my little horse's face and talk to him in this manner: "I wonder what we will see to day. take good care of me Billy and don't let me get hurt" he would bow his head as much as to say, he would do his best. . . . a day came when I had no pony to ride, the poor little fellow gave out. He could not endure the hardships of ceaseless travel. When I was forced to part with him, I cried until I was ill, and sat in the back of the wagon watching him become smaller and smaller as we drove on, until I could see him no more.

The grueling route hastened another loss. Luke Halloran, a bachelor, died of consumption on August 25. He must have looked like Virginia's grandmother by the end: gaunt, wasting away. But Halloran was only twenty-five. He had set out for California as "an invalid in search of health." His previous wagon train had abandoned him at the Little Sandy River, where Tamsen Donner took pity on him and took him in. Now she was helping to bury Luke in the Wasatch. His death was not a good omen.

Not even a gypsy could have drawn on her imagination & pictured half the trouble we wer[e] called upon to endure.

—Virginia Reed

⚬⚬⚬

CHAPTER 4

Losing a Home and a Father

Almost everyone in the Donner Party was from the flatlands of Illinois and Iowa. A spell of flat terrain might have made them feel better after the torture of the Wasatch Mountains. But they had never seen, felt, *suffered* flatness like that of the Great Salt Lake Desert.

Interstate 80 now cuts across this bleached swath of salt in Utah. It is one of those long, hot stretches of highway without towns or exits. People speed by in air-conditioned cars and marvel at the heat that shimmers in the nothingness. The area is so barren it is used as a U.S. government bombing range. Most people know it only for the Bonneville Salt Flats, where racecars have set speed records along the hard-packed straightaways.

The Donner Party had to cross this desert by wagon and on foot. They knew to expect blistering sun by day, then cold winds at night, because the desert has no trees or grass to hold the heat in. They steeled themselves for the total lack of natural shelter and water. What they didn't know was how long the "Dry Drive" would last. Forty miles, they estimated; three or four days.

As they were about to enter the desert, Tamsen Donner spotted a sign-

The Donner Party labored across the Great Salt Lake Desert for six long days. This marker points out their route. *(Marilyn Newton,* Reno Gazette-Journal. *Courtesy Nevada Humanities Committee)*

board and some scraps of paper. Like the diligent schoolteacher she had been, Tamsen pieced the bits of paper together: *2 days—2 nights—hard driving—cross—desert—reach water.* The note was from Lansford Hastings.

The company gave themselves and their remaining oxen a few days of well-deserved rest before setting out on the desert. The valley where they camped was beautiful. "Fine grass and water, and no one to molest us as the Indians were not troublesome," John Breen said later. "We should have wintered there."

Also, the desert crossing required planning. The men and boys cut grass and bundled it to carry along for the oxen to eat in the desert. The women and girls cooked. Finally, on September 1, they loaded the wagons with water. To carry enough for two days and two nights was impossible, mainly because water is so heavy. It weighs eight pounds a gallon, and the typical wagon could carry only two or three ten-gallon barrels, or thirty gallons at most. One ox alone, pulling a wagon, can drink twenty gallons a day. What little water they could transport would have to be rationed.

The desert must have seemed more alien than any terrain so far. The only living things, other than themselves, were the silent scorpions, lizards, and snakes that occasionally slithered by. The surface was hard, a combination of salt and alkali, where nothing can grow.

Soon the group was plagued by clouds of alkaline dust, raised by its own motion, which made it hard to see ten feet ahead. Worse, alkali is caustic; the fine powder settles into the skin and burns it. The travelers began to feel as if they had rolled in fire.

Then the oxen began to weaken. Salt and alkali were slow poison to them, on top of their extreme thirst. To Virginia "it seemed as though the hand of death had been laid upon the country," and that death might fall on the people, too.

Were they hallucinating a mountain in the middle of this desert? Even the soberest person had been imagining pools of water, desert mirages, for days. No, here was a real mountain, tough to climb at that. Energy rose as the company fought its way up, expecting and deserving to be rewarded at the summit with a vista of green trees and cool waters just beyond. The panorama was a shock: the desert stretched on.

The promise of "2 days—2 nights" was classic Hastings: as bad a miscalculation as his description of the Wasatch, a bitter joke.

The salt flats were mostly hard and dusty. Soon, however, came the sink, where the surface caved like rotten crust into a soft, brackish layer of muck beneath. The wagons labored in the soupy mess.

The heavily laden Reeds were trailing badly. And their water casks, like everyone else's, were just about empty.

When Reed lost control of a situation, his next step was almost always to saddle his horse. Virginia especially loved that part of her father—his readiness to spring into action. If William Graves and others disliked James Reed, she didn't care. She must have been comforted to see her father mount his horse and ride on to see where the desert ended.

What Reed saw along the way was alarming: most of his fellow travelers had unyoked their dying oxen and were driving them ahead to find water. Few sights were more sickening to people in wagon trains than seeing oxen die—it can be compared to losing the engine of a car. No oxen, no movement forward, except to walk to California.

Reed rode about thirty miles to reach the springs at the edge of the desert; the trip took eight hours. Those at the front of the group were almost out. Reed shouted words of encouragement to them on his return trip; they probably lacked the energy to answer him.

Reed returned to his family to find disaster. Apparently his eighteen oxen had been left untended by the teamsters for a few minutes. In that short time, all but two had stampeded into the desert, on a desperate search for water. Those two remaining animals, plus one sad cow, could not pull the family's three wagons. The Reeds were stranded. Virginia never forgot that day:

> Towards night the situation became desperate and we had only a few drops of water left; another night there meant death. We must set out on foot and try to reach some of the wagons. . . . Dragging ourselves along about ten miles, we reached the wagon of Jacob Donner. The family were all asleep, so we children lay down on the ground. A bitter wind swept over the desert, chilling us through and through. We crept closer together, and, when we complained of the cold, papa placed all five of our dogs around us.

A crazed ox bolted by in the dead of night. A black outline prancing against the starry horizon, it set the dogs to howling and the children to crying. The nightmare eased in the morning, as Patty Reed described:

> As soon as day light appeared, we went to [Jacob Donner's] wagon. . . . Mrs. Donner said . . . "Mr. Reed, let Mrs. Reed and the children stay with us and ride in our wagon." . . . We little ones were glad with the thought of riding with Aunt Betsy.

Death hovers over the "scene on the desert" included with other famous landmarks on an 1853 California travel brochure. *(The Bancroft Library)*

James Reed had to leave two wagons behind—probably the Pioneer Palace Car and one of the smaller rigs. There was no choice and no time to mourn. But Margaret, in particular, must have been devastated to abandon the family's comfortable chariot, their show of wealth, their only home.

Working quickly, Reed and his servants must have transferred their food and clothes into the remaining wagon. They removed the furniture and buried it as best they could, to prevent theft. "Caching," the emigrants called it. They spoke bravely of coming back to reclaim their goods.

A small irony caught Virginia's eye: ". . . when we left the poor old wagon on the planes [plains], as a monument to past comfort, the looking glass was not even cracked."

✤

Everyone suffered in the desert, although psychologically the Reeds may have suffered the most. The bedraggled Donner Party stumbled out, "mothers carrying their babes in their arms, and fathers with weaklings across their shoulders," as Eliza Donner recalled.

They walked to lighten the wagonloads of the starving oxen, whose ribs were showing, and to keep from spinning their wheels more than necessary. Even so, oxen were starting to drop dead. It was a dirty job to unyoke them and slaughter them for a few steaks. Sometimes the milk cows would be put under yoke in their place, a comical sight if it weren't so pathetic.

As a respite from thirst, Tamsen Donner gave all the children sugar lumps moistened with peppermint oil to suck. When those ran out, the children sucked on flattened bullets to bring forth a little saliva.

Sunburned and windburned, unbearably thirsty, they kept marching. Finally they reached water, at a site now known as Donner Springs, near Pilot Peak.

The agony ended after six days, not two days and two nights. Why anyone had believed Hastings's note was a mystery. Not that it mattered; they couldn't have carried much more water than they did, and in any case it had been far too late to turn back.

✤

No one knows if James Reed asked, pleaded, or commanded. But somehow he convinced the group to wait while he searched for his oxen. He was sure

Donner Springs provided the first water for the Donner Party after their desert ordeal.

(Marilyn Newton, Reno Gazette-Journal. Courtesy Nevada Humanities Committee)

they were hovering together in a canyon somewhere, if the local Indians—the Goshutes—hadn't killed them.

Reed couldn't find so much as a carcass.

Yet Reed's diary of September 9 indicates that he did return a few days later to salvage what was probably the Pioneer Palace Car. "Mr Graves Mr Pike & Mr Brin [Breen] loaned 2 Yoke cattle to J.F. Reed with one Yok[e] he had to bring his family wagon along," Reed noted. (He had the odd habit of often referring to himself in the third person, rarely as "I" or "me.") The Reeds still ended up losing two of their three wagons on the Great Salt Lake Desert; George Donner and Louis Keseberg abandoned one wagon each.

Twentieth-century archaeologists along all the emigrant trails have unearthed many pieces of wagons and pioneer goods. As late as the 1970s, excavators in the Great Salt Lake Desert were finding small items—like buttons and bullets—that dated to the Donner Party era. Any valuable items were long gone.

⁂

The company was still doggedly following the tracks of Hastings and the parties he was leading. They would never catch the man who had led them so far astray.

After the desert these tracks took them south, alongside some mountains. These were not the sierra; they came too soon and were too low. What was happening? Even Virginia's five-year-old brother knew California lay to the west, not the south. Was Hastings leading them to Mexico? Was he insane?

Eventually they understood. Hastings had done some exploring and found a slightly easier way over the small range called the Ruby Mountains. Unwittingly, the Donner Party did the same: two days south, then two days north, only to arrive within a few miles of where the unplanned detour had started. Four days were wasted when one day's hard climb would have done the job—a situation that couldn't have improved James Reed's popularity. All the women were "mad with anger," Reed noted in his diary in mid-September.

⁂

Finally, Hastings's "shortcut" led the Donner Party back onto the main route to California. They rejoined it at a well-known junction (near present-day Elko, Nevada) along the Humboldt River on September 26. The Humboldt was such an obvious landmark that even Hastings had gotten it right.

Usually, travelers could count on seeing at least a few other fellow emigrants at this spot. However, here and all along the Humboldt, it was as quiet as death. Most of the other wagons bound for California had passed this point a month ago. The people who went via Fort Hall were across the sierra already, or almost there.

Like a long, crooked finger pointing at the neighboring state of California, the Humboldt runs east to west across Nevada through sparse grass and sand hills. From there, the stages of the journey were well known: The river would end at a short but nasty lowland, the Humboldt Sink, then lead into a short desert. So another dry drive would precede the very hardest part of the trip: ascending the wall of mountains known as the Sierra Nevada.

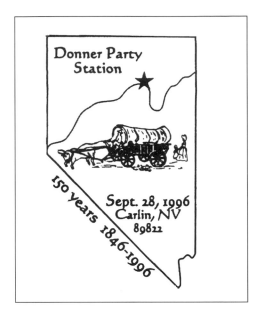

Carlin, Nevada, a small town on the Humboldt River, celebrated the 150th anniversary of the Donner Party's passing by issuing this one-day commemorative postmark. Hundreds of collectors from around the world sent in for copies. *(Author's collection)*

The Donner Party was already starting to run low on food. They couldn't exist solely on hunted meat. The only place to get provisions was ahead, in California, at the famous outpost of Sutter's Fort. Every emigrant had heard about the legendary generosity of John Augustus Sutter.

Sutter was an emigrant himself. Born in Germany of Swiss parents, he sailed to America at about age thirty and ended up, in 1838, traveling "with six brave men to Oregon, as I considered myself not strong enough to cross the Sierra Nevada." Sutter made his way south to California's fertile but largely empty Sacramento Valley.

There, under a land grant from Mexico, he planted crops, built a mill, and established a fort and trading post. And if John Sutter couldn't grow or manufacture something, he imported it. A master trader, he did business with Native Americans, the Hudson Bay Trading Company in Canada, and even the Russians, who would sail through the Bering Strait to San Francisco Bay, then journey inland the eighty miles or so to Sutter's Fort.

Fortified by cannons, Sutter's was like a self-sufficient city. It had its own army, composed mainly of Miwok men hired by Captain Sutter. And it had plenty of customers, including explorers, U.S. Army officers, soldiers, and emigrants.

(left) John Sutter
(Library of Congress)

(below) Sutter's Fort was like a small city, built within stone walls more than one foot thick. The fort (part original, part reconstruction) still stands in Sacramento; it is a state historic park.
(Denver Public Library, Western History Department)

The families of the Donner Party might have surrendered all their money to be at Sutter's Fort already. At least money could buy things there: blankets, hides, and fabric; cattle; grain and flour; and fresh fruits and vegetables. At Sutter's they could have slept in beds for the first time in six months and had their ailments tended—at no charge—by the physician whom Sutter generously kept on staff.

But money couldn't get the Donner Party an inch closer. The best they could do was send William "Mac" McCutchen and Charles Stanton ahead to Sutter's Fort to bring back food. The two must have made a comic sight, riding off side by side: big Mac, six and a half feet tall, and plucky Stanton, at least a foot shorter. Mac had volunteered to leave his wife and baby behind on this relief mission. Stanton had no family.

As rescuers, Charles Stanton (left) and William "Mac" McCutchen made an unlikely pair, and not just because of the difference in their heights. Stanton, born in Brooklyn, New York, was a bachelor who wrote poetry; McCutchen was a husband, father, and farmer from Missouri. *(Stanton, The Huntington Library. McCutchen, Author's collection)*

At least the Donner Party was finally moving fast, covering up to twenty miles a day along the Humboldt. They chose to separate temporarily into two groups. By camping in different spots each group would have more grass for the oxen and more animals for the men to hunt. The Donners took the lead. The strategy made little difference in the end, because hostile Shoshone and other Native Americans were now darting into both camps at night. They were from the various desert tribes known as Diggers. They stole the party's precious horses and oxen and shot arrows into their remaining livestock.

Days were growing shorter. So were tempers, especially among the men who took turns staying up nights to guard against cattle theft.

The route on October 5 led up a long sand hill. The trail grew narrow, causing a kind of traffic jam.

Milt Elliott, the Reeds' teamster, tried to pass John Snyder, the Graves' teamster, and the yokes of their oxen got entangled. They cursed each other, then Snyder lost control and began wildly beating the animals over the head. The families, on foot, must have watched in horror. Snyder was popular and usually a cheerful man.

James Reed came forward. Snyder screamed that he would beat him like a dumb ox, too. When Reed took out his knife, Snyder flipped the whip and lashed out with the heavy wooden handle. It tore into Reed's skull.

Reed stabbed squarely into Snyder's chest. Some observers thought he did it randomly, dodging Snyder's blow; others say that Reed aimed. According to some accounts, the high-strung Margaret Reed actually threw herself between the men, only to be knocked down by Snyder. Snyder did strike James Reed twice more.

With blood running into his eyes and mouth, Reed withdrew his knife, staggered to the river, and threw the knife in. The others watched Snyder die.

Virginia, not Margaret, was the one who calmly cleaned James Reed's face and dressed his wounds. She even had the intelligence to ask for a razor so she could clip the hair away from his cuts before swathing his head in bandages. Still, the event took its toll on her:

When my work was at last finished, I burst out crying. Papa clasped me in his arms, saying: "I should not have asked so much of you," and talked to me until I contained my feelings.

Meanwhile, the group angrily debated justice for Reed. Someone suggested taking written statements from the witnesses, so Reed could be tried for murder in California.

However, they weren't in the official United States anymore. This was unclaimed territory, and as the saying went: "Law doesn't travel west of the Missouri River." And no observer was impartial. Feelings against Reed already ran deep: Some blamed him for all their problems with the Hastings Cutoff. (They conveniently ignored that the majority had voted to take it.) Reed's high-and-mighty attitude rubbed more than a few people the wrong way.

Usually the captain of the party would intervene in a crisis. But the groups were still separated, with the Donners ahead by a day. Uncle George Donner, never a forceful leader, was not there to lead.

Everyone regrouped at sunset. According to legend, Louis Keseberg summoned James Reed forward. Early on, Reed had commanded Keseberg not to beat his wife; since then, Keseberg "hated my father and nursed his wrath," as Virginia put it. Now Keseberg sought revenge. He raised the tongue of a wagon to serve as a gallows to hang James Reed.

Was it a bluff? True, Reed had killed Snyder, but in self-defense. Others probably would have done the same. Virginia recalled the scene: her father "was no coward and he bared his neck, saying 'come on, gentlemen,' but no one moved" to hang him.

Some say that the idea for Reed's actual punishment came from William Eddy, one of his supporters. Or Reed himself may have made the suggestion. Either way, he was ordered to leave the group.

Reed hated to desert his family, but even he saw the wisdom of the banishment. He was far more useful riding ahead on the trail, not decomposing in a shallow grave, where his only value would be as dead meat for marauding coyotes.

Louis Keseberg
(Author's collection)

Assured by the group that his family would be cared for, Reed prepared to leave. He gave Margaret his most valuable items: a pocket watch and the silver medal that proclaimed his membership as a Master Mason.

Once again, Virginia did all she could to ease her father's way:

My father was sent out into an unknown country without provisions or arms—even his horse was at first denied him. When we learned of this decision, I followed him through the darkness, taking [Milt] Elliott with me, and carried him his rifle, pistols, ammunition, and some food. I had determined to stay with him, and begged him to let me stay . . . but he placed me in charge of Elliott, who started back to camp with me—and papa was left alone.

I had cried until I had hardly strength to walk, but when we reached camp and I saw the distress of my mother, with the little ones clinging around her and no arm to lean upon, it seemed suddenly to make a woman of me. I realized that I must be strong and help mama bear her sorrows.

Despair drove many frantic. Each family tried to cross the mountains but found it impossible.

—Virginia Reed

⟨〰⟩

CHAPTER 5

Rock upon Rock, Snow upon Snow

With James Reed banished, the group had a strange way of caring for his family.

Margaret Reed was informed, rather quickly, that her remaining wagon, the "family wagon" rescued by James Reed in the desert, was too burdensome to keep. This seems to have been presented crisply, as a group survival decision: Others had to abandon wagons, too, and the Reeds must continue to do their share by leaving the Pioneer Palace Car.

Margaret and Virginia must have wondered if there wasn't some spite involved as well, backlash against James Reed now that he was gone. *Wasn't it enough to have sent my husband away?* Margaret must have thought. *To have separated four children from their father?* Could the once-wealthy Reeds have nothing to call their own?

But if Margaret felt hysterical, it is unlikely she gave anyone the satisfaction of seeing it. A lady would not stoop to the level of people she found coarse. The bitterest truth was that she and the children were now dependent on others, in an atmosphere that was getting uglier by the day. They transferred their food and clothes into the Graves wagon, and the once-proud palace car remained behind like a skeleton.

Margaret still had hired hands to help her, including the invaluable Milt Elliott. But employees weren't quite like family, except in that they were mouths to feed.

The Reeds were left with two horses. Little Jimmy and Tommy rode on one; Margaret and the girls took turns on the other or walked beside.

"Every day we searched for some sign of Papa, who would leave a letter by the wayside," Virginia said. Sometimes they would also spot a cluster of feathers and rejoice that James Reed had found a goose to kill for food. They all worried about him, even three-year-old Tommy, who told his mother he didn't want to eat unless Papa was eating, too.

"But a time came when we found no letter and no trace of him," Virginia noted. By then, they were looking anxiously for James Reed's corpse. It was not an idle fear.

The two halves of the party moved faster and had more room at night to camp since splitting into two groups earlier in their journey. Eventually the rear group, with the Reeds, caught up to the Donners—and they quickly learned something awful. The Donners had come upon the remains of a man from Hastings's party. Paiute Indians had apparently killed him and come back later to pull his corpse from his grave. This they left on the trail, obviously as a warning. Sometimes at night the Donners thought they heard Indians laughing at them from the hills.

The Donners also had good news: James Reed was alive and no longer traveling alone. On catching up with the Donners, Reed had explained his banishment and that he was racing ahead to bring back help. The Donners insisted that teamster Walter Herron should go with him. Two men would be safer than one.

☙

On the whole, however, everything was breaking down.

On October 8, three days after Reed's banishment, the group abandoned not just a broken wagon but a sick person.

Hardcoop was his name, a Belgian-born emigrant so little known that his first name was not recorded. He had been traveling with the Kesebergs, who saw him as a burden and cast him from their wagon when no one else was around.

When the others realized what had happened, they pressed Louis Keseberg to turn back for the old man. Keseberg refused. As with the Reed–Snyder incident, he tended to see things in black and white; his ultimatum had been "Walk like the rest of us," and Hardcoop could no longer walk. *My wife and two children come first,* Keseberg no doubt reminded everyone.

William Eddy—who also had a wife and two young children—did some backtracking, to no avail. That night the group lit a giant bonfire, hoping Hardcoop might spot their camp and crawl in.

A few people talked about searching for Hardcoop the next day, but no one was willing to wait while they did. To some extent all of them, not just Louis Keseberg, were to blame for the abandonment.

William Eddy
(California State Parks,
Sutter's Fort State Historical Park)

Driven by the will to survive, the Donner Party sank to new depths. Not only did they leave Hardcoop behind—no doubt to die—but he would remain unburied. That had been unthinkable until now. Leaving a dead body exposed was what "savages" did, in their view—like the Diggers who had disinterred that man in Hastings's party.

The Humboldt River was not a pleasant stretch to travel. One pioneer called it "a filthy, mean, and muddy stream." The brown water moved as sluggishly as the pioneers did. There were virtually no trees to offer shelter and relief from the sun.

The Humboldt River ends at the Humboldt Sink, which the Donner Party reached by mid-October. The people who still had wagons almost certainly took the time to soak them in the river while they could. This was done to swell the wooden wheels, which were loose and full of cracks by this point. The ideal remedy would have been to grease the hubs and replace the spokes, but axle grease and wood were rare commodities by now.

Worse, another desert confronted the Donner Party at the Humboldt Sink. This time, at least, they had a better idea of what they were facing. It was

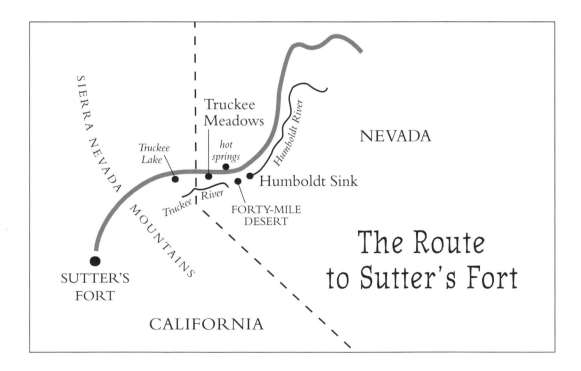

well known that this desert was forty miles long and took twenty-four hours to cross. Probably the party set out at noon and traveled through the night to take advantage of the cooler hours.

The Forty-Mile Desert, which stretches between today's towns of Fallon and Lovelock, Nevada, has been called Nevada's first ghost town. Coming so late in the westward journey, it was a make-or-break spot for many travelers. Generally the people survived, but their wagons didn't. The desert became a graveyard for abandoned wagons and for all the things that people couldn't carry without wagons: necessities such as stoves and kettles, and luxuries such as coffee grinders, violins, and roller skates.

The Forty-Mile Desert parallels this stretch near Carson City, Nevada, photographed in 1867. The surface was so powdery that wagons often spun their wheels in the sand. *(National Archives)*

The harshness of the Forty-Mile Desert forced pioneers to leave behind their wagons and all kinds of things in them. On display at the Churchill County Museum in Fallon, Nevada, are abandoned ox shoes (in the wooden frame), frying pans, barrel staves, and dozens of other relics. There are also many bones of animals that died in the desert, like the partially visible skeleton of a horse's skull with teeth intact. *(Marian Calabro)*

William Eddy lost his wagon at the start of the Forty-Mile Desert, after Paiutes had stolen or killed almost all of his oxen. He and his wife walked across, carrying their two babies. They shuffled through clouds of desert sand and alkali as fine as ash, looking across the horizon to jagged, uninviting out-croppings of rock. The Eddys had nothing at all left to eat or drink.

When they saw oxen and horses perking up and moving faster, they knew they were almost out. The animals could smell the hot springs at the desert's end before humans could.

The water did smell. But after forty miles of walking across a desert, it was all many people had to drink: hot sulfurous water from bubbling springs that smelled like rotten eggs. Legend has it that one of the Donner women gave Eddy some coffee grounds to mix with the water and mask its stink. Eddy didn't drink the coffee himself but used it to nourish his children.

People washed their clothes in this putrid water and hung them on the cottonwood trees to dry—the first trees anyone had seen for weeks. The area came to be called Ragtown for all the pioneer laundry done there.

⁓

Tensions were tightening, as another person in the Donner Party died.

Mr. Wolfinger, one of the German emigrants, was found murdered. His traveling companions, Augustus Spitzer and Joseph Reinhardt, blamed the local Indians. Others suspected that the companions themselves had murdered Wolfinger for the money and jewels he carried.

Doris Wolfinger did bury her husband.

An ugly dispute arose between William Eddy and Patrick Breen. The Eddys still had no food or water at all. William asked Patrick for water, not for himself, but for his toddler and infant. Breen had a good quantity of water, but he said no. He had seven thirsty children. Eddy promptly threatened to kill Breen and tapped his cask. Breen let him take all the water he wanted.

⁓

If ever a hero appeared in the nick of time, it was Charles Stanton. He arrived late in October with *food*. Dried fruit! Dried meat! Flour for bread! Bread was what everyone missed the most.

Although Stanton and McCutchen had headed to Sutter's Fort a month before, no one had counted on seeing them again—especially Stanton. As a carefree bachelor, would he really bother to return once he had crossed the mountains? McCutchen was different; he had left a wife and baby behind. But Mac was still at Sutter's, laid low by illness, and here was Stanton with desperately needed supplies.

Better yet, he wasn't alone. John Sutter had generously sent along two Native American employees, or vaqueros, of his, Luis and Salvador. These young members of the Miwok tribe knew the sierra well and could help keep the Donner Party on track.

A member of the
Miwok tribe
*(California State Parks, Sutter's
Fort State Historical Park)*

Stanton also brought the excellent news that James Reed and Walter Herron had arrived in California. Their journey had been tough: only three bites of food in the final seven days—mainly a few dried beans spilled days before from one of Hastings's wagons—followed by the death of Reed's horse.

However, Reed was organizing a rescue mission and would meet the Donner Party in the Sierra Nevada.

Hearing that, Margaret Reed probably felt she could withstand anything.

⟨ꙮ⟩

The company had joined the Truckee River at its bottomlands and followed it gradually upward to Truckee Meadows (modern-day Reno, Nevada). Previous white emigrants had named the area's features "Truckee" after the chief of the local Paiute tribe. The word means something like "very good" or "all is well."

Here was where the last long climb would begin: gradual at first, rougher every day. The company would end up fording the Truckee River at least twenty-two times. Still, following Stanton's arrival, tempers were improving.

William Eddy shot nine wild geese and shared them with everyone, even Patrick Breen.

Lulled by the good news about James Reed, and by their own full stomachs, the group promptly fell into old habits. They decided to rest for a few days. Actually, Stanton recommended it. Having just crossed the Sierra Nevada, which he deemed more treacherous than the brutal Wasatch Mountains, Stanton knew the company's broken-down oxen couldn't handle the very steep, rocky climbs that awaited them in the final fifty or so miles to the summit. To gain strength, the animals needed to feed as long as possible on the last rich grasslands at Truckee Meadows.

Treacherous terrain awaited the Donner Party as they left Truckee Meadows (modern-day Reno, Nevada) and entered the Sierra Nevada.
(Marian Calabro)

True, they were taking risks with the weather. Snow had already fallen atop the pass, but the people at Sutter's predicted the summit wouldn't be snowed in until mid-November. That was up to three weeks away—twenty-one days to cover only fifty miles. Any snow that fell in the meantime would surely melt within a day. And everyone knew that Lansford Hastings himself had made it over, with one day to spare, in the middle of the previous December.

A freak accident detained the group. William Pike's pistol accidentally fired just after he reloaded it and handed it to his brother-in-law. Pike took a bullet in the back and quickly died.

At age twenty-five, Pike was the Donner Party's first family man to die. He left a young widow, a toddler, and an infant. His death hit the group hard. It seemed more tragic than losing an old man like Hardcoop or even young bachelors like John Snyder and Luke Halloran.

Yet there was no time for grief. As people gathered around to bury Pike, the weather turned rainy. Hastily they threw dirt on his corpse and got away. Virginia understood that their race against time, weather, and hunger was far from over:

> We now packed what little we had left on one mule and started with Stanton. My mother rode on a mule, carrying Tommy in her lap; Patty and Jim rode behind the two Indians, and behind Mr. Stanton, and in this way we journeyed on through the rain, looking up with fear towards the mountains, where snow was already falling although it was only the last week in October.

Day after day they climbed. Fifty miles is an extremely long way up rocky terrain on foot and horseback. The mountain summit seemed as visible as the moon on clear nights, and about as far away.

ᎧᏗᏬ

The Donner Party was up against a wall: the long chain of mountains called the Sierra Nevada (Spanish for snowy range) which rises like a jagged wall barricading California from the land to the east. Millions of years earlier, arising from cracks and faults as far as six miles below the surface, pressure had forced the earth's crust upward. This movement created these mountains, as well as the surrounding deserts and sinks the Donner Party had to contend with.

These faults explain why eastern California has both the lowest and highest points in the United States (excluding Alaska). If fiery-hot Death Valley (282 feet below sea level) and snowcapped Mount Whitney (14,494 feet tall) were side by side, nearly twelve Empire State Buildings could be stacked between the valley floor and the mountain summit.

The mountain pass that threatened to trap the Donner Party is not the highest in the sierra; it is "only" 7,088 feet high. But mountains have natural weapons other than height. As Stanton warned, the Sierra Nevada is dauntingly steep, rocky, and wet on its eastern slope. It presents an obstacle course of sheer cliffs, rushing streams, and drifting snows. By contrast, the western slope is more gradual and forgiving—which is why the Donner Party was so eager to make it over the top.

Native Americans described the Sierra Nevada in their own way: "Rock upon rock," they warned the early explorer John C. Frémont. "Snow upon snow."

The higher the mountains, the more changeable and dangerous their weather. Mountain weather can kill. The peaks are like huge hands reaching into the atmosphere to capture moisture; when warm air collides with cool air, the result may be sudden bursts of blinding snow, rain, or fog. Virtually every wind that blows inland from the Pacific Ocean eventually slams into the wall of the sierra. Snow comes early there: heavy, wet snows called sierra cement fall with ruthless regularity and mount through the winter to depths of fifteen or twenty feet.

And winter, as Virginia observed, often starts in October.

⟨∞⟩

No one in the Donner Party was a stranger to snow. It snowed plenty in Illinois and Iowa and Germany, but never this early. Back home, they had watched snowstorms through their windows. Teams of plow horses had cleared the way around their farms or into town. Here they were picking

"Rock upon rock." Before railroad tracks were blasted through the Sierras, covered wagons had to navigate slopes like these. *(Denver Public Library, Western History Department)*

their way upward on mountain cliffs, open and exposed, in the middle of what felt like nowhere.

They encountered snowdrifts starting in the foothills, not far above Truckee Meadows. The cattle had to nose through the snows for grass. The more the group climbed, the higher the drifts became and the less likely to melt.

The Breens and Kesebergs understood the urgency and pushed the fastest—not that anyone could move very fast up the jagged slopes. The Reeds and most of the others, including Stanton and the Native American guides, were in the next group. The Donner families were lagging. Each day the group became more strung out, like beads on a necklace that could snap at any time.

As night fell on October 31, the first group finally reached Truckee Lake, a mere quarter mile below the crucial pass that was their doorway to California. There were five feet of snow on the ground, and the mountain summit was shrouded in thick clouds. Was more snow falling behind the veil of those clouds?

Truckee Lake, now called Donner Lake. This more recent photo (there were no electric lines in 1846), illustrates how the mountains hold snow even when the shoreline is bare. *(The Bancroft Library)*

The first group came to a cabin, which Stanton had told them about. Snowbound pioneers had built it the winter before. But they camped outside, in anticipation of a departure at dawn.

On November 1, clouds played hide-and-seek with the summit, revealing heavy snow on the pass. The first group made very slow headway, then lost the trail in fog. They were lucky to get back to the lake. The Breens were first to the cabin, and they took it over.

The second group, which included the Reeds, arrived around twilight with bad news. The Donner families had fallen far behind. Still pulling covered wagons, they had snapped an axle on a steep downhill and insisted on stopping to cut a tree trunk to replace it. In the process, George Donner had gashed his hand and lost a lot of blood.

November 2 brought drenching rain, the kind that falls in sheets. *Bad, but better than snow,* people probably told each other. *It will melt the snow. We'll wait it out.*

November 3 dawned with sun and blinding clarity: the rain at the lake had fallen as snow a mere quarter mile above. Virginia recalled:

All trails and roads were covered; and our only guide was the summit which it seemed we would never reach. . . .

When it was seen that the wagons could not be dragged through the snow, their goods and provisions were packed on oxen and another start was made, men and women walking in the snow up to their waists, carrying their children in their arms and trying to drive the cattle. The Indians said they could find no road, so a halt was called, and Stanton went ahead [with the Indians] . . . and came back and reported that we could get across if we kept right on, but that it would be impossible if [more] snow fell.

This time, no one moved. Instead, they ignited a dead pitch pine for a campfire and let the oxen roll on the ground and shed their packs.

Stanton, usually mild mannered, was furious. He, Luis, and Salvador had risked their lives to find the route; they had set tracks to the summit and back.

And the Miwok kept pointing to the ring around the moon: a forecast of big snows, they warned. Yes, everyone was worn out, but didn't they understand that this was their last chance to escape?

[Stanton] was in favor of a forced march . . . but some of our party were so tired and exhausted with the day's labor that they declared they could not take another step; so the few who knew the danger that the night might bring yielded to the many.

They gambled on being able to cross tomorrow. Would they be so lucky, given their lack of luck so far?

We camped within three miles of the summit. That night came the dreaded snow. Around the camp-fires under the trees great feathery flakes came whirling down. The air was so full of them that one could see objects only a few feet away. The Indians knew we were doomed. . . .

We children slept soundly on our cold bed of snow. . . . Every few moments my mother would have to shake the shawl—our only co-vering—to keep us from being buried alive.

In the morning the snow lay deep on mountain and valley. With heavy hearts we turned back.

A single overnight delivered a foot of new snow. Freezing winds whipped the snow into high drifts. The pass was impassable.

∾

If only they had stayed one less day at Truckee Meadows . . . or at the edge of the Humboldt Sink . . . or at Fort Bridger . . . or Weber Canyon. If only they had started one day earlier. . . .

One extra day would have gotten most of them over the summit. Not *out* of the mountains, but at least onto the western slopes, which were safer and more forgiving and within reach of the rescue parties.

Instead, the Sierra Nevada had slammed shut on the Donner Party like a prison door. Now, with little food but all the time in the world, they could contemplate these very smart words from Lansford Hastings's book:

Unless you pass over the mountains early in the fall, you are very liable to be detained, by impassable mountains of snow, until the next spring, or, perhaps, forever.

November 20, 1846: we now have killed most part of our cattle having to stay here untill next spring & live on poor beef without bread or salt   it snowed during the space of eight days with little intermission, after our arrival here.

—part of the first entry in Patrick Breen's diary

CHAPTER 6

Trapped in the Depths

The group turned back to Truckee Lake. The lake was pretty, but not to their eyes: It reflected the mountain they couldn't cross, the snow-covered peaks that kept them hostage, and the blue sky that often turned dark with new storms.

To be trapped in the mountains, to endure subzero temperatures at night, to face the likelihood of starving or freezing to death—this knowledge must have stirred the deepest terror. But the emigrants didn't sit and cry. They began building homes for the winter. After all, they had a chance. James Reed's rescue party was still on the way.

Today, people frequently ask why the Donner Party didn't just turn back to the warmer area of Truckee Meadows, fifty miles east. They couldn't turn back for the same reason they couldn't go forward: too much snow.

The Breens had first claim on the cabin that already stood near the lake. It was about sixteen feet by twenty feet, with a fireplace and chimney. The walls were ox hide and pine brush; the floor was dirt. The only things inside

View of Truckee Lake (Donner Lake) from the summit. The Donner Party encountered far more snow than is shown here. When the pioneers couldn't cross the pass, they trudged back to the lake and prepared to spend the winter. *(Library of Congress)*

were books—a Bible, a volume of Shakespeare, *The Life of Daniel Boone,* and others—apparently left behind by the emigrants who built the cabin a year or two before. There was no furniture. There were no windows, because there was nowhere to get glass.

The Kesebergs erected a lean-to, or three-walled shack, against one end of the Breen cabin. The others built from scratch, cutting trees for two log cabins. Quite deliberately, they built them a fair distance apart. It was a good half-mile walk between the farthest cabins.

The Reeds and their hired hands, along with Stanton and the Native Americans, shared half of one new cabin. The Graves family, with their seven children, lived in the other half. A wall separated the two halves, and each side had its own door, so the occupants did not have to cross paths. This was a blessing for Margaret, because the Reed and Graves families were not on the friendliest terms.

The other new cabin was erected against a large granite rock. The rock acted as wall and chimney for a row of fireplaces. The space was about twenty-five feet long by eighteen feet wide by eight feet high, roughly the dimen-

This old sketch of the Truckee Lake encampment was based on a description by William Murphy, who was trapped there. On the left is the Graves-Reed double cabin, with its roof of ox hides and two separate doors. On the right is the Breen cabin, with its slanted roof. Keseberg's lean-to is beside it. The triangle near the lake is an inexact rendition of the rock that formed one wall of the cabin that housed the Eddys, Murphys, Fosters, and Pikes. *(The Bancroft Library)*

sions of a modern two-car garage. The cabin housed the Murphys, Pikes, Fosters, and Eddys.

After framing the cabins, the next task was to slaughter most of the surviving oxen. Their hides would be used, with branches and canvas, to roof the cabins. Indeed, from the minute the oxtails went into the soup kettle, no part of the animals went to waste. "The cattle were all killed, and the meat was placed in snow for preservation," Virginia said.

The frozen meat, like everything along the way, was not community property. Each family carefully monitored its own hoard. Hunger drove hard bargains: "My mother had no cattle to kill," Virginia recalled, "but she made arrangements for some, promising to give two for one in California." The only currency of real value was not money, but dead oxen.

Although the emigrants had little food, at least they had unlimited water. The lake wasn't frozen solid at first, and snow could be always be melted in kettles over the fire. There were plenty of trees to chop down for firewood, if you could get to them as the snowdrifts grew. The drifts were starting to become taller than the cabins themselves.

⌒⌳⌒

George and Jacob Donner and their families were not at Truckee Lake. After George's accident, they had never caught up to the others. They were camped at Alder Creek, five or six miles back.

Margaret Reed probably missed the Donners. Her friends from Springfield might not have had much to share, but maybe they wouldn't have made her bargain and beg like the others did.

The grim reality was that the Reeds, like almost everyone else, had only ox meat and flour left to eat. A total of 81 people were trapped at Donner Lake and Alder Creek: 25 men, 15 women, and 41 children. Twenty-two of them would try once more to cross the summit in late November, only to fail and return to the camps. Five would die of starvation and illness by Christmas.

The Breens alone had a decent store of food, but with seven children in their family it wouldn't last forever. And Patrick Breen was suffering from kidney stones, a painful malady. As he tersely noted in his diary on Christmas Eve: "Poor prospect of any kind of comfort, spiritual or temporal."

Nine days before Christmas, in fact, the situation was so dire that fifteen of the strongest emigrants set off for help. Most of them were young people without children. If they had to die, they decided, at least they would die trying to get help. Franklin Graves, a native of Vermont, made them snowshoes for the journey.

This group, then simply called "the snowshoers," later became known as the Forlorn Hope. Mary Ann Graves, age twenty, took part because "the cries of hunger from my brothers and sisters was more than I could stand." The snowshoers also included two of the party's most determined men, Charles Stanton and William Eddy, as well as Luis and Salvador, who knew the Sierra Nevada well.

Among them, too, was Patrick Dolan, the laughing Irishman who had danced the jig at those happy campfires back on the plains. He was not so merry in the days before his departure, as Patty Reed recalled: "Mr. Dolan

Mary Ann Graves
*(California State Parks,
Sutter's Fort State
Historical Park)*

demanded security from my Mother for beef which she bought from him." Margaret Reed had to surrender to Dolan what were perhaps her last two mementos of her husband, his pocket watch and Mason's medal.

"I was a going with them [the snowshoers] & I took sick & could not go," Virginia later reported. It must have been a moment of wishful bravado. Her mother never would have let her go, and Virginia loved her family too much to leave.

With the Forlorn Hope on its way and James Reed still presumably alive, there were at least two faint possibilities for rescue.

⟋⟍⟍⟍⟍⟋

The Donner families were even worse off than those at the lake, at least physically.

Shortly before Christmas, the Reeds' teamster Milt Elliott hiked the five or six miles to Alder Creek to check on the Donners. He found tents that looked like wigwams. Probably because the elderly Donner brothers lacked the strength even to build crude cabins, they had simply chopped down some slender tree trunks, propped them against a standing tree trunk, then draped torn canvas and quilts over the frame. Their teamsters did the same.

Snow piled on these tents, almost caving them in. The walls of fabric were always wet. The people at Alder Creek wore damp clothes, walked in wet shoes, and slept in damp beds; nothing had a chance to dry.

By Christmas, Jacob Donner and three of the teamsters were dead. The cut on George's hand had gotten infected and the infection was eating its way up his arm.

However, the families of the Donner brothers did share what little they had, and it made a difference. Jacob's widow, Betsy, and George's wife, Tamsen, were coping well. And their twelve children and stepchildren seemed content, with the girls putting snow into cups and pretending to have tea parties.

Even the toddlers made their own amusements. "A little sunbeam stole down and made a bright spot upon our floor," Eliza Donner remembered later. The daughter of George and Tamsen, Eliza was just three years old that winter. Playing with the ray of sun was one of her first memories. "I sat down under it, held it on my lap, passed my hand up and down in its brightness. I

The George Donner Tree at Alder Creek. A marker commemorates it as the tree that supported his family's tent shelter. Historians and archaeologists now think that the camp was a short distance away, on land since covered by the Prosser Reservoir.

(Marian Calabro)

gathered up a piece of it in my apron and ran to my mother. Great was my surprise when I carefully opened the folds and found that I had nothing to show."

As matters got worse, the Donners were reduced to gnawing on ox bones "burned brown" and eating "some of the few mice that came in camp." Tamsen, a gifted teacher, turned to the Bible for storytelling and consolation. Eliza said: "While knitting and sewing, [my mother] held us children spellbound with wondrous tales of Joseph in Egypt, of Daniel in the lion's den . . . and of the Master who took young children in His arms and blessed them."

⁂

Here is the entry from Patrick Breen's diary on Christmas Day: "Began to snow yesterday about 12 o clock snowd. all night & snows yet rapidly . . . Great difficulty in geting wood . . . offerd. our prayers to God this Cherimass morning the prospect is apalling but hope in God Amen."

⁂

For the Reed children, Christmas brought a near miracle.

Virginia, Patty, Jim, and Tommy stared into the kettle at the best sight they had seen in a long time.

Food was bubbling in the water. It was real food, not the nauseating broth made from boiled hides of oxen that had become their daily fare.

A handful of beans, half a cup of rice, a few dried apple slices may have been a snack once, but they were a feast now.

Most exciting of all, there was meat. From a secret hiding place, Margaret Reed had produced a square of bacon about the size of the palm of little Jim's hand. She had also saved a bit of tripe, the honeycomblike stuff that had lined the stomach of one of the slaughtered oxen.

Beans, rice, apples, bacon, tripe. These now-luxurious items were simmering in the pot together, sending up a warm, succulent steam that mixed with the dank smells of the cabin. Whenever a morsel of bacon rose to the surface, the children filled the room with cheers.

Last Christmas they had been in Springfield. Their maid, Eliza Williams, had probably served up huge roasts, bowls of vegetables, hot loaves of bread, and more pies and cakes than anyone could eat. The abundance of food was not the only painful memory. James Reed had been there, of course—where else would he have been, a father at the head of the family table on Christmas day?—and so had their late grandmother.

Yet this year's meal was also lavish, in its own way. Its ingredients could have been stretched into a month's worth of thin soups. But from the very day they were trapped by the snows, on November 4, Margaret had vowed she would give her family some happiness on Christmas.

Milt Elliott joined in the celebration. The young man had stuck by the Reeds through their miseries and felt like a part of the family. He even called Margaret "Ma." Eliza Williams was on hand, too, but she barely functioned as a maid. Her half brother Baylis had just died, and Eliza may have been losing her mind from hunger.

In the cold and dirty cabin, lit and heated only by fire, the disheveled group said grace and thought their own thoughts. As she served the stew, Margaret said words she would not say again for a long time: "Eat slowly, for this one day you can have all you wish."

The usual daily fare, soup made from ox hides, was making them all gag. The recipe was to cut the hides into strips, burn off the hair, then boil down the leathery skin for hours and let it cool. The result was a jellylike "pot of glue" that even the adults found hard to swallow. Only the Breens, who needed it least, didn't seem to mind it.

People often ask (with great frustration) why the families didn't hunt and fish. They had guns, and no doubt tried to shoot game, but the only targets seem to have been mice. If foxes or coyotes passed in the day, they probably moved too quickly to be shot. Deer had migrated to lower elevations. Fishing also proved useless once the lake froze. The emigrants tried ice fishing but weren't really equipped for it.

Early on, as legend has it, William Eddy shot a grizzly bear for meat. (In the 1980s, archaeologists unearthed burnt grizzly bear bones near the Truckee Lake encampment.) But grizzlies and black bears den up for the winter, so they weren't a feasible source of food.

In any case, the weather was too cold to spend whole days moving around in the open, especially as people grew weaker and sicker. Also, the frequent blizzards and mounting snow made movement just about impossible, even with snowshoes. There were five feet of snow on the ground in November and twenty-two feet by March—which means that the snow rose higher than a two-story building.

"The game had left the mountains, and the fish in the lake would not bite," Eliza Donner later summarized.

"No liveing thing without wings can get about," Patrick Breen wrote.

∽

The Murphy children actually ate a rug. It was made from some sort of animal skin and was drying out in front of the fire. They discovered by chance that they could break off pieces and toast them. The crispy bits went down more easily than the boiled hides did.

Others, in desperation, boiled the leather from shoes and book covers to eat.

Sickening as those hides and bits of leather must have been, the Reeds

A fanciful illustration of William Eddy hunting a bear *(Author's collection)*

missed them when they were gone. By New Year's they had to sacrifice the children's pet, Cash. (Apparently the other four dogs had died along the trail.) The cooked body of the little terrier sustained them for a full week. They even boiled down Cash's bones to chew. "We ate his entrails and feet & hide & evry thing about him," Virginia later reported. Patty remembered it, too, in her breathless way:

> A poor little dog, saved us, from, death of hunger . . . dog! is good! any way! or where! you may try! don't, doubt, me . . . this is true . . .

After eating Cash the Reeds had almost nothing, and Margaret had to make her hardest decision yet. With Milt, Eliza, and Virginia, she would try to cross the mountain. The other children were too small to come along. Margaret still hoped to meet her husband on the other side.

They set out on January 4, a springlike morning, leaving their cabin on a path that was surrounded by such deep snow that it was more like a tunnel. "May God of Mercy help them," Breen wrote in his diary. "Tom [remains behind] with us   Pat with Keysburg & Jas [James] with Graveses folks. It was difficult for Mrs. Reid [Reed] to get away from the children." To keep the little ones from trying to follow, said Virginia, "we told them we would bring them Bread & then thay was willing to stay."

Eliza stumbled back to camp the next day. The others returned after four nights, on snowshoes Milt made along the way. Of course they brought no bread. Their compass had broken. Virginia knew just how lucky they were to be back: "That same night thare was the worst storme we had that winter & if we had not come back that night we would never got back."

The phrase "eating themselves out of house and home" is usually an exaggeration, but for the Reeds it was fact. They had to start removing the ox hides from their roof to cook them. Margaret hacked off pieces each day, fighting an impossible battle between hunger and shelter.

One day Elizabeth Graves insisted those hides now belonged to *her,* as payment for the ones Margaret borrowed earlier. Perhaps two women have never hated each other more than these two. They still harbored bad feelings over James Reed's killing of John Snyder, who had been a friend of the Graveses and possibly Mary Ann's fiancé.

The journey to California had already cost Margaret her home, her mother, all her worldly goods, and possibly her husband. Had it come to this, now? Starved and fighting over ox hides? Apparently so.

"The Graves seized on Mrs. Reids goods untill they would be paid," Breen wrote in his diary, noting that Mrs. Graves did leave the Reeds with two hides. These may have been hides from the roof, or perhaps Margaret finally took some that Patrick Dolan or Charles Stanton had left behind.

"You may know from these proceedings what our fare is in camp," Breen noted. *And our mood,* he might have added. Breen's diary is mostly notes about the weather and daily conditions, not people, but Mrs. Graves drew a rare personal comment: "She is a case." Mercifully, the Breens helped the Reeds. "When the hides were taken off our cabin and we were left without shelter,

Patrick Breen's diary, February 6–8, 1847:

Satd 6th it snowed faster last night & today than it has done this winter & still Continues without an intermission   wind S.W.   Murphys folks and Keysburgs say they cant eat hides. I wish we had enough of them   Mrs Eddy very weak

Sund. 7th   Ceased to snow last [night] after one of the most Severe Storms we experienced this winter   the snow fell about 4 feet deep   I had to shovel the snow off our shanty this morning   it thawed so fast & thawed during the whole storm. today it is quite pleasant   wind S.W.   Milt here today says Mrs. Reid has to get a hide from Mrs. Murphy & McCutchins child died 2nd of this month.

Mond 8th   fine clear morning   wind S.W.   froze hard last [night]   Spitzer died last night about 3 o clock to[day] we will bury him in the snow   Mrs Eddy died on the night of the 7th *(The Bancroft Library)*

Mr. Breen gave us a home," Virginia recalled. The Reeds, with Eliza, moved into the Breens' cabin.

Virginia had come back to camp on her hands and knees, her feet crippled by frostbite. Her prospects for survival were not good. However, Peggy Breen had always liked the girl, and she risked her husband's fury by slipping her bits of food. Patrick had housed the Reeds; he couldn't feed them too. But he softened. "Mr. Breen would cook his meat; we used to take the bones, heat them up, boil them and boil them over and over again," Virginia said.

The families made an effort to bury their dead, placing the bodies in the ever-deepening snowdrifts. As teenager John Breen said: "Death had become so common an event that it was looked upon as a matter of course, and we all expected to go soon." John and his brother Edward, whose broken leg had mended well, did the burying because they were the strongest.

On February 9, they buried Milt Elliott. Just a few days earlier, Milt had been desperately bargaining on Margaret's behalf for another hide from Levinah Murphy—with no luck. Now he was gone, and his small supply of food was his last legacy to the family he loved.

John Breen, a teenager, helped to bury the dead. It was sadly easy work, he said, "because they were so light from starvation." *(California State Parks, Sutter's Fort State Historical Park)*

Virginia helped bury him. "Commencing at his feet, I patted the pure white snow down softly until I reached his face. Poor Milt! it was hard to cover that face from sight forever, for with his death our best friend was gone."

In body and especially in spirit, the Reeds were failing.

"Mrs. Reid has headache," Patrick noted in his spare way on February 13. Two days later: "Mrs. Graves refused to give Mrs. Reid any hides"—again. And the day after that: "We all feel very weakly to-day."

⌘

Soon, people were also breaking down their homes from the inside. They began chopping off pieces of the log-cabin walls to stoke their fires. This was because snowdrifts sometimes blew against the door and made it impossible to go outside and cut wood. Other times, the men would cut timber but be unable to lift it when it fell into deep snowdrifts.

As time crept on, the sameness of the days was numbing. At the beginning, the families sat and talked so they could "some times almost forget one-selfs for a while," in Virginia's words. Then sitting became difficult, because they had lost all the fat on their bottoms. People would lie motionless for hours to conserve what little energy they had.

Always the strongest, with their seemingly endless supply of food, Patrick and Peggy Breen began to read aloud from their Bible and prayer book. They invited the others to join in. Soon their cabin hummed with readings and prayer. Here was one thing that the Irish Catholic immigrants and the wealthy Illinois Protestants could wholeheartedly share: a cry to God to save them. *O Lord, hast Thou forsaken me?*

The cabin was dark, lit only by flickering flames. Eight-year-old Patty Reed loved the ritual of lighting candles (actually little twigs) and praying. "All of us that were out of bed would kneel to hear & feel—God have mercy!" she later wrote. Images of angels, devils, and life everlasting captivated Patty to the point where she seemed to go into a trance, which is also consistent with extreme hunger. If her mind was in another place, perhaps she couldn't feel the eternal, damp cold and smell the constant odors of the windowless cabin—the sickening steam of bones boiling in the kettle, the wet earthen floor, the unwashed clothes, babies whose cloth diapers were mere shreds.

Virginia prayed and watched. "I never think of that cabin but that I can see us all of the ground, praying. I can see my Mother planning and wondering what else she could do for her children."

Sometimes Virginia went outside to lie on a blanket in the sun, as they all did. It wasn't much colder in the open, and there was light. She read *The Life of Daniel Boone* again and again. It seemed miraculous that this particular book was there. Daniel Boone, an early pioneer from Kentucky, had lived among Native Americans and hacked his way through hostile territory, just like the Donner Party, and he had survived.

But the plagues of the Bible, which Virginia could also read, seemed closer to their own hardships that winter.

ᨮ

Sometime in February, Virginia felt herself slipping away:

> We had all gone to bed—I was with my mother and the little ones, all huddled together to keep from freezing—but I could not sleep. It was a fearful night and I felt that the hour was not far distant when we would go to sleep—never to wake again in this world. All at once I found myself on my knees with my hands clasped, looking up through the darkness, making a vow that if God would send us relief and let me see my father again I would be a Catholic.

Virginia revived. Later in the month, John Breen saw something that seemed like a vision:

> One evening, as I was gazing around, I saw an Indian coming from the mountain. He came to the cabin and said something which we could not understand. He had a small pack on his back, consisting of a fur blanket, and about two dozen of what is called California soaproot. . . . He appeared very friendly, gave us two or three of the roots, and went on his way.

What was this visitor telling them? How frustrating that no one could talk with him! He must have seemed like a figure from a dream. Luis and Salvador might have spoken his language, but they were away with the Forlorn Hope, which had now been gone for two months.

The gift was ironic. Soap plants have roots that can in fact be used like soap—something the emigrants needed. But they are also edible, so the emigrants ate them. They "taste like sweet potatoes," Patrick Breen wrote. But the really curious point of the visit is that the Native Americans knew that the emigrants were there.

Almost forty years later, in her book *Life Among the Piutes,* Sarah Winnemucca, the granddaughter of Chief Truckee, the leader for whom the Truckee River was named, told how her tribe quietly kept tabs on the strangers in their area:

Sarah Winnemucca was the granddaughter of Chief Truckee of the Paiute tribe and an accomplished leader in her own right. "I was a very small child when the first white people came into our country," she wrote. "They came like a lion, yes, like a roaring lion, and have continued so ever since, and I have never forgotten their first coming." *(Nevada Historical Society)*

Those were the last white men that came along that fall. . . . white people perished in the mountains, for it was too late to cross them. We could have saved them, only my people were afraid of them. They must have suffered fearfully . . . the snow was too deep.

"The Sierra Nevada is rock upon rock, snow upon snow," as Sarah Winnemucca's people had warned the first white people who ventured there. Despite the small gift of food, the group at Truckee Lake was starving. And though they didn't yet know it, the severity of the mountains had driven their friends and relatives in the Forlorn Hope to break the final taboo: They had begun to eat their own dead.

They had begun perhaps, as they looked about with maniacal cravings for food, to regard their comrades as offering certain new possibilities. Man might eat beef—good! Man might eat horse, too, as the need came, and mule. He might eat bear and dog, and even coyote and owl. He might also—and the relentless logic drove on—yes, man might also eat man.

—George R. Stewart in *Ordeal by Hunger,* a history of the Donner Party

We could not help it. There was nothing else.

—Georgia Donner, a survivor

CHAPTER 7

The Last Taboo

The first people in the Donner Party to engage in cannibalism—the eating of human flesh—were members of the Forlorn Hope, the group of ten men and five women who left Truckee Lake in mid-December to seek help.

Estimating it was thirty miles to the first settlement in California, and that they could cover five miles a day, the snowshoers had packed six days' worth of food. *Food* is a generous term; each person's daily rations were a few strips of dried beef, a bit of coffee, and sugar. To keep their packs light, they brought no changes of clothing and only one blanket each.

Their miseries could fill a separate book. They experienced "snow upon snow" as they tried to cross the sierra. When the storms ended and the sun came out, it was to torture them. Many experienced snow blindness, a temporary dimming of vision caused by the reflection of ultraviolet rays off the vast whiteness all around them. Some days they could barely see to walk.

Nature seemed to have a bottomless bag of cruel tricks to play on this group, which included some of the youngest and strongest adults of all the pioneers. The jagged, icy surface of the snow tore their snowshoes apart. They followed streams that seemed to run west but that really ran southwest, leading them away from their destination.

Out of food by the sixth day, the snowshoers were nowhere near the Sacramento Valley. And their unofficial leader, plucky Charles Stanton, became the first among them to die. If the Donner Party has an untarnished hero, it is Stanton. Safe at Sutter's Fort back in October, with no family ties to anyone in the party, he could have easily stayed in California. Yet he kept his promise and returned to the mountains with help. Stanton's reward turned out to be death. At least he died peacefully, sucking his pipe as he sat by the fire.

"Leaving the weak to die." This artist's depiction, created for *Century* magazine in 1891, evokes the deaths of John Denton and Charles Stanton. Both were said to have died quietly by a fire. *(Author's collection)*

It is likely that thoughts of cannibalism flickered in a few minds. But to devour Stanton, of all people? No one could speak of it.

Then a kind of miracle happened. Feeling weak and looking to lighten his load, William Eddy rummaged through his pack. Amid packets of gunpowder and tobacco he discovered half a pound of bear meat, accompanied by a note signed "your own dear Eleanor." It was a secret gift from his wife, who had stayed behind.

Eight ounces of bear meat, not much bigger than a hamburger but more deliciously fatty, kept fourteen people alive for a few more days. Once again, however, there was nothing. And the once-jolly Patrick Dolan broached the grimmest subject imaginable, the thing everyone was thinking but none dared mention—the possibility of eating the dead. "Even the wind seemed to hold its breath as the suggestion was made that were one to die, the rest might live," said Mary Ann Graves.

Eleanor Eddy
(California State Parks,
Sutter's Fort State Historical Park)

Were one to die, the rest might live. Should they kill someone, then? They discussed it. Wanting the sacrifice to be fair, Dolan suggested drawing lots. Eddy, the unofficial leader after Stanton's death, had another idea. How about drawing two names at random, for a shootout? It seemed more fair for a person to die fighting. Certainly it was more fair to Eddy, who was the best marksman.

The talk led nowhere, in the end, if only because it was too gruesome a subject for Christmas Day.

The group decided to wait for someone to die naturally. That would be soon, by the look of things.

As if a greater power had heard the depths to which they would plunge, the Forlorn Hope had its worst night yet. Ice and snow rained down on them. They packed down the existing snow, which was ten to fifteen feet deep, and made their customary little fire. Then they did their nightly maneuver to capture body heat: they huddled together in a circle around the fire and drew their blankets over the group like one big tent. They poked a tiny hole for the smoke to escape, and the fire heated the inside of their "tent" as the falling snow landed on their backs and further insulated them.

That night, however, the huddle slowly started to sink. The fire overheated the snow beneath them, and down they began to go, creating icy water all around as they submerged. They might melt through twenty feet of snow before hitting ground and never be able to crawl out—if they lived at all.

In the group's panic, someone upset the fire and put it out. Patrick Dolan started to hallucinate and broke free. Perhaps, recalling the happy early days of the journey, he was trying to dance the jig again. His Irish brogue faded in the pitch-black night as he died. Eerily, in rapid succession, three others succumbed to starvation and cold. (They were a cattle herder named Antonio, teenager Lem Murphy, and Franklin Graves.)

Amid the chaos, William Eddy desperately sought order. Stumbling over bodies in the snow and dark, Eddy tried to light a fire with gunpowder. He only burned himself badly.

Were one to die, the rest might live. Patrick Dolan's words must have echoed in many minds the morning after his death. On December 26, he became the first to be cannibalized. While some of his friends lit a fire, others cut the flesh from Dolan's thin, dead limbs. At that point they had not eaten anything for five days. They are said to have sobbed and covered their faces as they roasted and ate Dolan's body.

William Eddy could not bring himself to partake. Neither could Luis and Salvador. The three abstainers took a walk together, away from the drifting smell of the fire.

∽

The Forlorn Hope violated the deep-seated taboo and discovered that it did not kill anyone. Quite the opposite. Their bellies almost sickeningly full with human flesh, they stayed put and gained strength for three days. Like the efficient farmers they had been, they butchered and stripped the three remaining dead bodies of their hearts, livers, and brains. After eating all they could stomach, they dried the rest of the meat to take with them as they moved on.

Cannibalism is such a last resort that there are few recorded instances of it in recent history (apart from rites of vanishing tribes). Yet whenever it happens in survival situations—on shipwrecked boats or deserted islands—an instinctive rule comes into play. Members of a family try not to eat their own dead. Two of the dead had relatives still living among the Forlorn Hope. So, almost without discussion, the group took pains to identify and distribute the cooked flesh carefully. It lasted them one week, followed by three more days without anything to eat.

What happened next may be the most shameful part of the entire Donner Party saga.

William Foster wanted to kill Luis and Salvador for food. Maybe he blamed them for the fact that the Forlorn Hope was still lost and wandering; they had come from Sutter's Fort and were supposed to know the mountains. Like many whites of the time, Foster may have felt that Native Americans were expendable.

By at least one account, William Eddy stood up to Foster. He reminded him that these men had saved their lives in October by bringing food from Sutter's Fort. He pointed out that the snowshoers had already rejected the idea of slaughtering people in cold blood for food—a far different thing from eating the dead from sheer necessity.

William Foster
(California State Library)

Eddy also alerted Luis and Salvador to Foster's plan. They promptly ran away.

During the next few days, Eddy may have killed a deer, which kept the group fed for another few days. (Eddy later claimed that he did; other survivors of the Forlorn Hope never mentioned this.) At any rate, the group was soon out of food again.

Some tragic fate was hovering. The group crossed paths with Luis and Salvador, who were dying. Despite some protests, Foster quickly murdered the Native Americans.

Eddy and the women in the group hid their faces as Foster's shots rang out; they would not witness such an act. Foster and the two women in his family partook of the dead bodies. The others claim to have abstained.

William Eddy's feet were frostbitten to a bloody pulp, but he dragged himself on. The others were close behind. They half-walked, half-crawled to a small settlement of Native Americans, probably Miwok or Maidu, who fed them pine nuts and acorn bread.

These rescuers guided Eddy to a small group of emigrants, some from Illinois, who were wintering in Bear Valley, forty miles north of Sutter's Fort. To see Indians delivering a skeletal white man in the dead of winter must have shocked them. Quickly they took over. The pioneer women washed Eddy's raw feet. The men followed his bloody tracks in reverse, found the rest of the Forlorn Hope, about six miles behind, and led them to safety.

In mid-January, after thirty-three days, the journey that should have taken six days finally ended. All five women in the Forlorn Hope survived. Only two of the ten men did: William Eddy, who befriended the Native American rescuers, and William Foster, who murdered them. Eddy wrote a letter about the Donner Party and the Forlorn Hope that soon reached Sutter's Fort. It horrified everyone there—the news was far, far worse than they had imagined.

⟋⟍⟋

From Sutter's Fort, two rescue parties were finally mobilizing to move east. James Reed led one. Aquilla Glover led the other. Glover, who had emigrated the year before, had known the Donners and Reeds in Illinois.

Reed had helped organize and raise the funds for both rescue teams, which had not been easy. Most of the likely candidates were fighting the war against Mexico. Many were skeptical that anyone in the Donner Party was still alive, and they didn't want to risk their own lives finding out.

Reed himself ended up volunteering to fight in the Battle of Santa Clara on January 2, trying to defeat the Mexicans more quickly and raise goodwill among potential rescuers. He also traveled to San Francisco, then called Yerba Buena, to drum up recruits. He even convinced a few sailors to come along. Perhaps, like Virginia Reed, these men had never seen mountains and were eager for the new experience.

(Busy as he was with rescue efforts, James Reed lost no time in pursuing free land. Besides filing his own claims, he forged applications for at least two others, signing as Margaret Reed and Baylis Williams. He also managed to be put in charge of Mission San Jose and began planting crops there.)

The war ended on January 10, 1847, when the U.S. Marines took Los

Angeles from the Mexicans. On January 31, Aquilla Glover's rescue team was the first to start out.

Three of its ten recruits, however, turned back. They decided that no amount of money could compensate for slogging through twenty feet of snow with seventy-five-pound packs on their backs—not even their amazing salary of three dollars a day, later raised to five dollars for those who persevered.

At sundown we reached the Cabins and found the people in great distress such as I have never witnessed there having been 12 deaths and more expected every hour   the sight of us appeared to put life into their emaciated frames.

—Reason Tucker, first rescue team

⌘

CHAPTER 8

Rescued at Last

After almost three weeks on the trail, trudging through deep snow by day and camping on it by night, Aquilla Glover and six rescuers caught sight of their destination. The date was February 18. James Reed's team was still on its way.

Moving as fast as possible on snowshoes, Glover's team crossed the summit and headed downhill toward the lake. They could see curls of smoke rising from the cabins, indicating that fires were burning within, but the camp appeared empty. "At sunset we crossed Truckee Lake on the ice. . . . We raised a loud hello," recalled Daniel Rhoads. He and his brother, John, both Mormons, had sworn to rescue the Donner Party or die trying.

People began to emerge slowly from cabins and from holes in the snow. The pioneers sometimes spent daylight hours in this way, outside their windowless cabins, cocooning themselves into the insulating snow and turning their faces to the sun. To the rescuers, they seemed like the dead rising.

"They were gaunt with famine," Rhoads said, "and I can never forget the horrible, ghastly sight they presented."

Four separate rescue teams saved the Donner Party. This sketch of the first, based on survivors' descriptions, is by the same artist who depicted the Truckee Lake encampment *(see page 90)*. The lake is now frozen and snow-covered—the rescuers have just crossed it on snowshoes—and the cabins are almost buried in snow. *(The Bancroft Library)*

And in their numbness or near delirium—for many were quite close to death—the pioneers could not trust the vision before them. "The first woman spoke in a hollow voice," said Rhoads, "very much agitated."

"Are you men from California?" she asked. "Or do you come from heaven?"

⌘

Rescuers had to guard the food to keep people from taking too much and possibly gorging to death. The desperate emigrants were stealing everything they could find: "They even stole the buckskin strings from the party's snowshoes and ate them," one rescuer recalled.

Rescuer Reason "Dan" Tucker hiked to the Donner family tents at Alder Creek. He was greeted by one of the Donners' hired hands, teenager Jean Baptiste Trudeau, who was probing the snowdrifts with a long stick.

Clearly Tucker had arrived with food just in time. The young man explained that if he couldn't find a forgotten ox to thaw and cook, the Donners would be forced to eat the dead—probably not for the first time.

(right) Daniel Rhoads, photographed years after the rescue. He and his brother John joined the first rescue team because "not to make any attempt to save them would be a disgrace to us and California, as long as time lasted." *(California State Library)*

(left) Reason "Dan" Tucker was an 1846 emigrant who had briefly traveled with the Graves family. He took part in the first rescue with his son George, age sixteen, and returned with the fourth rescue team. Dan witnessed the reunion of the Reeds in the mountains, on February 27. He wrote in his diary: "Mr. Reed met with his wife and two children the meeting was very affecting." *(Author's collection)*

At both camps, people pressed the rescuers for news of the Forlorn Hope. They were told only that the snowshoers had been detained by badly frost–bitten feet. Glover knew their exact fate, however, which was why he had coached his men to lie. If those still trapped learned the whole truth—about the six-day trip that took thirty-three days, about how eight of the fifteen had perished—they might just have given up then and there.

⁓

Not everyone could leave with the first rescue party. Glover had stored food along the trail for the return trip, but it wasn't enough to feed all forty people still alive at the two camps. As Patrick Breen noted with typical understate-ment in his diary: "7 men arrived from Coliforcia yesterday evening with som provisions but left the greater part on the way."

The Reeds were among those who left first. All of them, Margaret especially, were longing to meet James Reed in the mountains. (Glover had predicted that Reed and his rescue team were just a few days behind.) The Breens sent out their sons Edward and Simon. The rest of that family stayed behind, still possessing enough food to tide them over.

At Alder Creek, Tamsen and Betsy Donner volunteered to remain with their younger children. They didn't want to abandon Tamsen's husband, George, who clung to life despite the massive infection in his arm.

On February 22, four days after they had arrived, Glover's men led seven adults and sixteen children toward the summit. What happened within a few miles was another blow to Margaret Reed's heart. Her three-year-old son, Tommy, simply could not walk on the trail of packed snow that the rescuers had created. His short legs sank into the adult footprints; each step was a climb. Yet no one could, or would, carry him in their arms on a journey that might last a week. His own mother lacked the strength.

After conferring with Aquilla Glover, Margaret agreed to send Tommy back, with Patty to look after him. Glover would deliver them to the Breens with a minimum of food for their keep. Margaret trusted Glover because he was a Mason, as her husband was.

Patty sized up the situation quickly. Four days shy of her ninth birthday, she had already experienced more than most people do in a lifetime. Like

Margaret Breen and some of her children during the difficult second rescue, as later imagined by an artist for *Century* magazine, 1891 *(Author's collection)*

Virginia, she was more concerned about her mother than herself. "Ma, if you never see me again, do the best you can," Patty said in farewell.

"That was the hades [hardest] thing yet," Virginia said. "The men said they could hardly stand it, it made them all cry but they said it was better for all of us to go on."

⌘

Waiting for the second rescue party, even the well-stocked Breens were starting to run out of possibilities. Their pet dog, Towser, finally went into the kettle. Others had passed that point and were moving, at last, to the extreme.

The first mention of cannibalism at Truckee Lake appears in the February 26 entry of Patrick Breen's diary: "Mrs. Murphy said here yesterday that [she] thought she would commence on Milt and eat him. I don't think that she has done so yet, it is distressing."

But soon Levinah Murphy and her family did butcher Milt Elliott's body—dead and frozen for over two weeks—to eat his heart and liver.

The Murphys had no way of knowing that the Forlorn Hope had also resorted to cannibalism, two months earlier. Nor did they know that cannibalism had begun at Alder Creek, on the dead bodies of Jacob Donner and some of the families' employees, including Samuel Shoemaker. (One example lingered in the memory of four-year-old Georgia Donner, who remembered decades later how her Aunt Betsy "came down the steps one day saying to my mother, 'What do you think I cooked this morning?' Then answered the question herself, 'Shoemaker's arm.'")

Those who cannibalized seem to have observed the instinctive rule: they carefully identified the remains so that people would not have to eat their own relatives. Under this code of honor the Donners might have cannibalized less, because many people at Alder Creek were related.

ᏬᎿᎧ

More bad luck followed Virginia's group of refugees as they struggled to find their way out of the mountains and into the sunny valleys of California.

Wild animals had eaten the food carefully cached by the rescuers, so the group divided what little remained in their packs and sent two men ahead for more. They were climbing a "great hye mountain as strait as stair steps in snow up to our knees," in Virginia's words, on a daily ration of one ounce of smoked beef and two spoons of flour.

Five-year-old Jimmy Reed was barely better off than Tommy had been. "James walk the hole way over all the mountain in snow up to his waist," Virginia marveled. "Poor little fellow, he would have to place his knee on the hill of snow between each step of the snowshoes and climb over; he was too small to reach from one step to the other." The boy's persistence made him a favorite. The rescuers assured Jimmy that life would be better in California. His pa would buy him a horse, they assured him, and Jimmy would never have to walk anywhere if he didn't want to.

"We were, Mother and I, very much afraid that he would give out," Virginia wrote. It was a realistic fear; another small child had just died. "We had talked the matter over and had desided what we would do; we encouraged him in every way, kept telling him that every step he took he was gitting nearer Papa."

That promise, at least, would soon come true. After six days, the group had finally crossed the mountain pass and scaled the wall of snow that trapped them. They were still in the mountains, to be sure, struggling through snowdrifts, hemmed in on narrow paths. However, James Reed and the second rescue party were only a few miles away.

⚬⚬⚬

"Is Mrs. Reed with you? Tell her Mr. Reed is here."

Thus the ever-formal James Reed announced himself to an advance member of Glover's party. Virginia and her mother were more emotional. After all, they had been separated from James Reed for four torturous months:

> My mother dropped on the snow. I started to run to meet him, kept falling down, but finally was folded in my dear Father's arms once more. "Your mother, my child, where is she?" I pointed towards her. I could not speak. . . .

Soon Reed and his men were surrounded. Later that day, he recorded the scene in his diary:

> I can not describe the death-like look they all had. Bread Bread Bread was the begging of every child and grown person except my Wife.

In anticipation of this moment, James Reed had baked bread. The pioneers tore into it.

The day was not so happy for William McCutchen, the Donner Party member who had set off for Sutter's Fort with Charles Stanton back in October. "Mac" had returned as part of Reed's rescue team. He anxiously scanned the group for signs of his wife and baby but learned they had died.

The Reeds' reunion had to be brief. "When my father heard that Pattie and little Tommie were still in the mountains, he could hardly stop long enough," Virginia later wrote. "He was so much afraid something would happen, or they would die before he could reach him." Reed and the other rescuers quickly moved on to Truckee Lake.

With renewed energy, the survivors continued to Johnson's Ranch, the first white settlement west of the sierra. Here at last was the California that Virginia had been promised:

> We were out of the snow, could see the blessed earth and green grass again. How beautiful it looked. We stayed a day or so, gitting the horses and mules ready to ride [to Sutter's Fort]. Just think of it, to ride. . . . No more dragging over the snow, when we were tired, so very tired, but green grass, horses to ride, and plenty to eat.

For one teenager, a stepson of Jacob Donner, "plenty" was too much. A body in starvation is easily strained; it can process only small amounts of food at first. William Hook found a cache of food, secretly ate all he could, then died in agony trying to digest it. His death was a warning to the others to go slowly.

⌒⌒⌒

On March 1, Patty was sitting in the sun on the cabin roof when she spotted her father and nine other rescuers approaching. She cried out happily, but fell as she ran toward him; she was very weak.

Inside the cabin, Tommy was near death. James Reed fed and bathed him. He also bathed Louis Keseberg, the man who had once wanted to hang him.

Two days later, the children were stronger. Patty was able to take on a pleasant job just before the second group left, as Eliza Donner recalled:

> Mr. Reed's little daughter Mattie [Patty] appeared carrying in her apron a number of newly baked biscuits which her father had just taken from the hot ashes of his camp fire. Joyfully she handed one to each inmate. . . .

The "inmates" departed on March 3, but not all of them. A dozen or so stayed behind, many because they were too weak to move. Tamsen Donner was in decent shape but would not be parted from her dying husband, so she remained with her three little girls. This final group would wait for a third rescue team, or die waiting.

No one escaped easily. After two days on the trail the emigrants faced a blizzard, described by James Reed as:

> A Hurricane [that] has never ceased for ten minutes at a time during one of the most dismal nights I ever witnessed . . . at one time our fire was nearly gone and had it not been for Mr McCutchen's exertions it would have entirely disapeared . . . the little half starved half frozen poor children would say I'm glad I'm Glad we have got some fire Oh how good it feels, it is good our fire didn't go out. . . .

One child died, and others—including the Breens—were too weak to continue. Deciding to wait along the trail for a third rescue party, they would be forced to live in a snow pit and watch some of their members die—and to cannibalize.

However, the Reeds and five others pressed on. James Reed was so worried about the dwindling supplies that he scraped the seams of the empty food sacks and saved the crumbs in the thumb of a mitten.

Patty was weakening, but insisted on walking until she dropped. "I see angels and stars!" she cried out in a stupor. Her father revived her with the hidden crumbs, and carried her the rest of the way to Johnson's Ranch. Soon they would be reunited with the rest of the family and put the nightmare behind them.

⌒⌒⌒

William Eddy had recovered well enough to lead a third rescue party. Ironically, it included the only other male survivor of the Forlorn Hope, William Foster.

These two men, once enemies, forged a tragic bond on arriving at the cabins. The thought of rescuing their families must have sustained them as they trudged back through the mountains that had almost killed them. They found the worst sight possible: their wives and young sons, for whom they had returned, were dead and cannibalized.

A horrible thought struck Eddy and Foster—they suspected that Louis Keseberg might have cold-bloodedly killed their boys, not even waiting for them to die naturally.

There is no evidence that Keseberg murdered anyone for food. Still, it is easy to imagine the rage and despair of the two fathers, who had already been through so much. Eddy swore revenge on Keseberg; he vowed that he would kill him if both of them managed to make it to California.

Would Eddy and Foster have rescued Keseberg, given the sickening circumstances? It didn't matter: Keseberg was too sick to travel now. He would have to survive on his own; his wife had gone ahead with the first rescue party. Levinah Murphy, the forceful widow who had been the first to cannibalize at Truckee Lake, couldn't tend him, either. She was too ill to move.

Eddy's group ended up rescuing only young Simon Murphy and the three little Donners: Frances, age six; Georgia, age four; and Eliza, age three. The girls' mother, the smart and vibrant Tamsen, had to choose between accompanying them or staying with her elderly, dying husband.

Tamsen stayed. Perhaps she felt that her children were safe with others, but only she could nurse her husband. Exactly what prompted her decision is one of the great mysteries of the Donner Party. Tamsen kept a diary during the journey, but no one ever found it.

George Donner died the day after the rescuers left. Levinah Murphy died soon after. Some people believe that once these potential witnesses were gone, and eaten, Keseberg felt free to kill Tamsen Donner to keep himself alive.

Did he murder her? Did he burn her diary, which would have been a fascinating and invaluable record of the entire journey? Did Tamsen burn it herself? One of her daughters recalled her mother shredding bits of paper to kindle a fire in the ordeal's darkest days. These are mysteries never to be solved.

There is no question, however, that Keseberg prevailed. In April, a fourth rescue team arrived. What they found, according to rescuer William O. Fallon's reports, included books, calico cloth, tea, coffee, shoes, ammunition, household goods, and kitchen furniture. The body of George Donner was carefully wrapped in a clean white sheet. Tamsen Donner's body was nowhere to be found. "We were obliged to witness sights from which we would have fain turned away, and which are too dreadful to put on record," Fallon said.

The rescuers escorted Louis Keseberg, and Keseberg alone, over the mountain.

⚬⚭⚬

Group by group, the survivors made their way to Johnson's Ranch, then to Sutter's Fort, to recover. For the first time in many long months they could enjoy the simple luxuries of warmth, dry clothes, and restful sleep. Like Virginia, they could appreciate the "blessed earth and green grass again . . . and plenty to eat."

⚬⚭⚬

With the last survivor rescued, the final numbers could be tallied. The Donner Party numbered ninety in all: eighty-eight emigrants, plus Luis and Salvador, the Miwok who joined the group in October. (Some historians put the total at eighty-nine, preferring not to count Virginia's grandmother, Sarah Keyes, because she died early in the trip and of natural causes.) Eighty-one were trapped in the mountains.

Of the ninety people, forty-seven survived and forty-three died.

Six of the deaths took place before California, and two just after reaching safety. (One of the latter was the unfortunate boy who ate too much food too quickly.) The rest of the victims died in the snows, either while entrapped or during rescue attempts.

Curiously, the death rate was much higher for men and boys than for women and girls. Of the fifty-five males in the full group, more than half of them died: thirty-two in all. Of the thirty-five females, about a third died: eleven in all. Fifty-eight percent of the males died, while only thirty-one percent of the females perished. Women were almost twice as likely to have survived.

One possible explanation is social. While some men in the group were unattached, all of the women and girls traveled in families, which provided support. Many of the women, like Margaret Reed and her daughters, were mothers and older sisters who were fighting to stay alive for the sake of their young ones. "The mothers were the real heroes," Patty Reed later said.

However, the men, regardless of marital status or age, also fought for survival—for themselves and others. More men than women went on rescue missions, for example. That exposed them to more risk and, in turn, to a higher chance of death.

Another possible reason for the women's higher survival rate is physiological. Females, especially after maturity, typically have more body fat than males and thus more reserves to draw on. And because they are usually smaller than men, they require less food to subsist.

Age also mattered—the chances of survival were better for the young, but not the youngest. Of the ninety participants, forty-three were teenagers and children, of whom about two in three survived. Most of the young people who died, ten boys and five girls, were under five years old. Their tender age may explain their vulnerability to hunger, illness, and extreme cold.

Survival, however, was bittersweet for many of the young survivors. More than half of them lost both parents and arrived in the golden land of California as orphans.

In the end, only two families made it to California with no loss of life at all: the Breens and the Reeds.

Of the forty-three teenagers and children, almost two out of three survived. Billy Murphy, ten years old during the winter of 1846–47, was a survivor. *(California State Parks, Sutter's Fort State Historical Park)*

We are all very well pleased with Callifornia. . . . it aut to be a beautiful Country to pay us for our truble giting there.

—Virginia Reed, May 1847

⌇

CHAPTER 9

Looking Back, Looking Ahead

Three months after leaving Truckee Lake, Virginia Reed composed a long letter about the Donner Party. Very few correspondents in history have had so much to tell.

Virginia, almost fourteen, was writing to a cousin back in Springfield. She wrote to Mary Keyes on May 16, 1847, while at Yount's Ranch in Napa Valley, a short distance north of San Francisco. After two months at Johnson's Ranch and Sutter's Fort, the Reeds were staying at Yount's temporarily while James Reed arranged the family's future life.

Reproduced on pages 165–171, Virginia's letter is as brilliant as its spelling is inventive. Her words capture what the journey was like and how things turned bad. There is probably no better summary of the entrapment than hers:

The snow was so deep we could not go over & we had to go back to the cabin & build more cabins & stay thar all winter without Pa   we had not the first thing to eat . . . we stoped thare the 4th of November

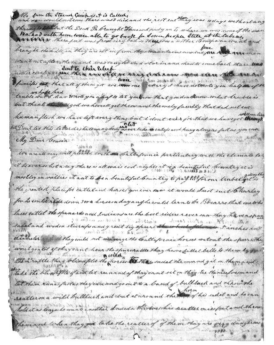
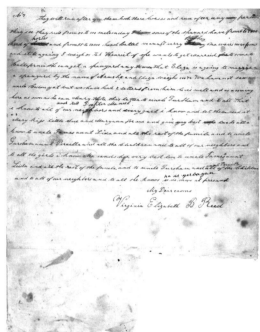

Virginia Reed's letter. James Reed added the corrections between some lines. Sixty-five years later, Virginia looked back: "My very first scribble, poor old letter—I did not think it would live so long. I promised a cousin of mine that I would write and tell her all about our [journey] when we reached California—little I thought what I would have to tell." *(The Bancroft Library)*

> & staid till March and what we had to eat i cant hardley tell you . . . o Mary I would cry and wish I had what you all wasted.

Of Lansford W. Hastings, whose shortcut proved to be so disastrous, Virginia said little: "thay pursuaded us to take Hastings cutof over the salt plain   thay said it saved 3 Hundred miles." It is not clear who "thay" were. Maybe Virginia was trying to forget that her father had been one of the "persuaders," or protect him from future blame.

Surely it was loyalty to James Reed that stopped Virginia from reporting on the murder of Snyder and her father's banishment. She told half the truth: "pa had to go on to Callifornia for provisions."

Oddly, she did not dwell on the sad fate of the Pioneer Palace Car: "in 2 or 3 days after pa left we had to cash [cache] our wagon and take Mr graves wagon and cash some more of our things." The loss of the luxurious wagon may have seemed small, given the tragedies that followed.

O my Dear Cousin you dont now what trubel is yet.   Many a time we had on the last thing a cooking and did not now wher the next would come from but there was awl weis some way provided   there was 15 in the cabon we was in and half of us had to lay a bed all the time   thare was 10 starved to death then   we was hadly abel to walk we lived on little cash [the dog] a week.

Virginia had nearly died when she and her mother tried to escape. Yet she did not dramatize her suffering. All she told her cousin was: "I froze one of my feet verry bad."

Of the actual rescue, Virginia wrote mostly of the sadness when her little brother and sister had to turn back. Her description of meeting her father in the mountains is a masterpiece of understatement:

O Mary you do not now how glad we was to see him we had not seen him for 6 months   we thought we would never see him again   he heard we was coming and he made some s[w]eet cakes to give us   he said he would see Martha and Thomas the naxt day.

Virginia was aware of the cannibalism, even though she was not present when it happened. She is matter-of-fact about the Forlorn Hope: "thay lost the road & got out of provisions & the ones that got throwe [through] had to eat them that Died."

Of those who cannibalized at Truckee Lake and Alder Creek, Virginia wrote: "some of the compana [company] was eating them that Died   but Thomas & Martha [Patty] had not ate any."

Seeming to realize even then that the Donner Party would forever be branded as cannibals, Virginia took pains to separate her family from the oth-ers. She didn't blame anyone for deeds done from necessity, but she also didn't want anyone to regard the Reeds as ghouls. So she emphasized once more to Mary that hers was "the onely family that did not eat human flesh."

Yet Patty and Thomas Reed might have done so, without knowing it. Until their father rescued them, they stayed with the Breens, who may have cannibalized. Peg Breen might have supplemented the Reed children's scanty supply of food, just as she once slipped bits of ox meat to Virginia.

In the end, however, "eating them that Died" was not the most important thing—at least to Virginia. She understood what really mattered.

"Thank god we have all got throw," she wrote to Mary. "We have left everything [behind] but i don't cair [about] that   we have got throw with our lives."

⁊⁊⁊

Patty Reed never wrote a letter like Virginia's, but she gave the world her own mementos of the Donner Party. After being carried to safety at Johnson's Ranch, Patty unwrapped three precious items that she had hidden in her clothes for months. Probably even Virginia hadn't known they were there.

Patty's carefully preserved treasures were a glass salt shaker from Springfield, a lock of her grandmother's hair, and a small wooden doll. She kept them secret so that no adult could force her to abandon them.

The original doll is on display in Sacramento at Sutter's Fort, which is

Patty Reed's doll

(Nikki Pahl/California State Parks, Sutter's Fort State Historical Park)

now a state historic park. (A replica is on display at the Emigrant Trail Museum at Donner Memorial State Park in Truckee, California.)

James Reed had given his pocket watch and silver Masonic medal to his wife when he was banished. She, in desperation, traded them to Patrick Dolan for food for her children. But the items made their way back to the Reeds after Native American employees of John Sutter found them on Dolan's corpse. Today they are also on display at Sutter's Fort

Other tangible objects survived the Donner Party ordeal. The Bancroft Library at the University of California at Berkeley, for example, has an early photographic copy of Virginia's letter (the original was lost), the diaries of Patrick Breen and James Reed, and other invaluable items. But they are not on public view like the doll, watch, and medal, which give a face to the Donner Party legend.

∞

About a month after Virginia wrote her letter, General Stephen W. Kearny of the U.S. Army led troops to Truckee Lake on a cleanup mission. The group included people with more than a casual interest in the task. There were Edwin Bryant, who had traveled west with the Donners and Reeds part of the way and had sent back the warning letter never delivered to them at Fort Bridger; William Fallon, one of Louis Keseberg's rescuers; and teenager William Graves, a survivor of the Donner Party.

It was June 22, technically summer, but the drifts on the summit were still deep enough to require snowshoes. The snow at the encampment had melted, but the ground was soft and wet.

Canvassing the area, Kearny and his men found body parts, fragments, and human bones. Even for tough soldiers, these sights were hard to take. "A more revolting and appalling spectacle I never witnessed," said Fallon.

According to Edwin Bryant, the soldiers dug a mass grave, and buried the long dead. Then one lit a match:

> The cabins, by order of Major Swords, were fired, and with every thing surrounding them connected with this horrid melancholy tragedy, were consumed.

Later, people passing the area would find that the soldiers did an incomplete job. Apparently only the Breen cabin was completely burned by Kearny's men, and no evidence of a mass grave has ever been found. Perhaps the mission horrified the soldiers so much that they hurried away from what they saw.

This rock *(above)*, which formed one wall of the Murphy cabin, is all that remains of the Truckee Lake encampment. The bronze marker *(detail, left)* honors those who perished and those who survived. The rock now faces a visitors' trail in Donner Memorial State Park.

(Marian Calabro)

Although postal service did not yet exist in the West, Virginia's letter did reach Mary Keyes. Edwin Bryant carried it with him on a return trip to Springfield that summer. Mary's parents took the letter to the local newspaper, the same one in which George Donner had advertised for hired hands before the trip began. In December, it appeared under the headline "Deeply Interesting Letter." (The editors didn't rush to publish it because the big news at that time was the rewriting of the Illinois state constitution.)

Without telephones, radio, or TV, the news traveled by newspaper, letter, and word of mouth. *The California Star* began publishing lurid reports of the Donner Party as early as February 1847, after William Eddy's letter reached Sutter's Fort. Those pieces reached Oregon within two months and spread east to Missouri and Illinois by autumn. Within a few years the Donner saga was written into two books as well, Jessy Quinn Thornton's *Oregon and California in 1848* and Edwin Bryant's *What I Saw in California.*

News spread slowly and unevenly in those days, however. As the Donner

"A more shocking scene cannot be imagined." *The California Star,* a San Francisco newspaper, was quick to publish horror stories of the Donner Party. Other newspapers around the country reprinted them. These lurid, often inaccurate accounts made the participants sound like ghouls. *(Author's collection)*

Party was being rescued in the late winter and spring of 1847, others who had never heard of them were innocently starting the same journey.

Still, the lessons of the Donner Party did affect emigration in 1847 and 1848: only 850 people moved to California in those two years, down from 1,500 in 1846. The numbers headed for Oregon picked up by several thousand.

But all fears soon disappeared when an emigrant from New Jersey discovered gold at Sutter's Mill, near Sutter's Fort. Reports of the glittering wealth in "them thar hills" lured almost seventy thousand overland emigrants to California in 1849 and 1850. (Tens of thousands more came by sea, sailing from the East Coast around South America to San Francisco.) Free gold sounded even better than free land, and the gold rush was on in full force.

Numbers of Overland Emigrants

YEAR	OREGON	CALIFORNIA
1840	13	—
1841	24	34
1842	125	—
1843	875	38
1844	1,475	53
1845	2,500	260
1846	1,200	1,500
1847	4,000	450
1848	1,300	400
1849	450	25,000
1850	6,000	44,000

Source: End of the Trail Museum, Oregon City, Oregon

Some of the forty-niners came by way of what was already being called Donner Pass. Many others had a healthy distrust of it, thanks to the Donner Party. They followed longer but safer routes over other sierra passes. When the winter of 1849–50 threatened to be as bad as that of 1846–47, the U.S. Army quickly sent out rescue squads. The tragedy of the Donner Party would not be repeated.

Not even the promise of gold, however, could tempt many forty-niners onto the Hastings Cutoff. By then, most people knew it was no shortcut. Also, Lansford Hastings had stopped promoting it. After a spell of lawyering in San Francisco and other ventures, he gave up his wild dream of becoming California's leader. Hastings's final frontier was South America; he ultimately urged emigrants to move to Brazil, just as he had once tried to sell them on California.

In 1850, California became the thirty-first state. Each year, it grew easier to reach. In the 1850s, people began to emigrate in horse-drawn stagecoaches,

The building of the Central Pacific Railroad across the Humboldt Desert. Huge teams of laborers, mainly Chinese immigrants, raced to finish the job in 1867. *(Denver Public Library, Western History Department)*

reaching San Francisco from the Midwest in a few weeks rather than months. By the Civil War in the 1860s, when James Reed's old war comrade Abraham Lincoln was U.S. president, the wealthy were making the journey for pleasure. They had full-time cooks by day and farmhouse beds to sleep in when they stopped at night.

Then the Central Pacific Railroad was completed in 1867, followed by the Union Pacific Railroad two years later. Linking the eastern and western United States for the first time, the trains cut the transcontinental trip to six days—an eternity now, but the blink of an eye before highways and cars existed. (Hundreds of Chinese laborers died building the rails across the Sierra Nevada, but their tragedy is a separate story.)

Unknowingly, the Donner Party cleared a path for another famous group of pioneers. By hacking a route through the Wasatch Mountains—the tedious cutting of trees and moving of boulders that slowed them down so much—they enabled thousands of Mormons to reach the Great Salt Lake in Utah more easily the very next year. The Mormons, whose religious migration is yet another chapter in the history of the West, later paid tribute to the Donner Party by depicting their labors on a sculpted monument in Salt Lake City. The Mormons of 1847 weren't tempted to try Hastings Cutoff, however, because they had already been warned about it.

⌒⊙⊙⌒

The section of the Sierra Nevada that stopped the Donner Party now commemorates them. Truckee Lake is called Donner Lake. The mountain peak is Donner Summit. The path over it is Donner Pass.

Donner Pass is a wide ribbon of concrete now. After the railroads came in, the old wagon trail was neglected until cars came into use. The trail, first paved in 1909, is now part of Interstate 80. The road builders of 1964 took longer to cross Donner Pass than the emigrants of 1846–47 did: It took them five years to complete ten miles of freeway across the granite cliffs. That section gets so slippery in winter that tire chains are often required to drive it. Sudden storms also close the pass from time to time, leaving drivers sitting in their heated cars and feeling terribly inconvenienced.

Amtrak's New York-to-California railroad route also crosses Donner Pass,

(left) The granite boulders of the Donner Summit area as viewed from the train
(Marian Calabro)

(below) Interstate 80 westbound at Donner Summit. A sign just beyond says "Steep Downgrades Next 40 Miles."
(Marian Calabro)

on tracks that cling to the sides of the mountains and pass through long, dark tunnels blasted through rock. A volunteer historian usually comes aboard at Truckee, a town close to the Donner Pass, to narrate the tale of the Donner Party. Californians, who are well versed in natural tragedies such as earthquakes and mudslides and fires, seem to take pride in hearing about the Donner disaster again and again.

Marcia Savin, a San Francisco native who has frequently made this rail journey, says: "When the Zephyr makes the long climb to Donner Pass and the unearthly blue of Donner Lake suddenly breaks through the dense trees, a hush comes over the car and we hear the story again. It has such a hold on us, I think, because unlike most pathfinders, the Donners and Reeds weren't explorers or scientists but ordinary families, with their children and dogs and in-laws. Ordinary people crossing the mighty sierra in winter, on wagons and on foot. It was so foolhardy and so brave. All of us California schoolchildren learned about their wretched end. But what is more amazing is that some of them survived to tell the extraordinary tale."

Near the top of Donner Pass is Donner Memorial State Park. At first glance it seems like any state park, with a campground, picnic grove, lakefront beach, and boat launch. But it is also an entry point to the Emigrant Trail, used by hikers and cross-country skiers. Markers commemorate the rock against which the Murphy cabin stood. (The Graves cabin site is commemorated with a cross on nearby Donner Pass Road, where gas stations and outlet stores have all but swallowed it up.) A museum at the park tells of the experiences of the Donners, Reeds, and other emigrants.

The museum also displays some buttons, bone fragments, and other items unearthed near the encampments. Archaeologists have long searched for relics from the Donner Party. While they have unearthed hundreds of items from the period, none can be linked directly to the Donner Party. The most tantalizing find was an 1839 coin from England's Isle of Man, which may have belonged to British-born Donner teamster John Denton. There was also a hoard of buried American coins found in 1891, which the Graves family claimed. They identified the coins as theirs because their babies had teethed on them.

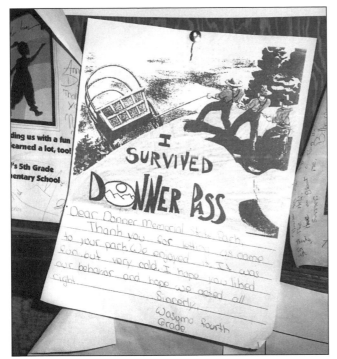

(below) Elizabeth Graves hid her family's gold coins at Truckee Lake just before leaving with rescuers. She died a few days later and the hiding place remained unknown until 1891, when the hoard was discovered. *(The Bancroft Library)*

Some of the excavated items at the Emigrant Trail Museum come from Alder Creek, where the Donner families wintered. That area, which has a good interpretive trail, is open to the public as part of Tahoe National Forest. It is located within the unfortunately named Donner Memorial Picnic Site.

The main attraction of Donner Memorial State Park is the large monument to the Donner Party. Its base is twenty-two feet high, the exact height of the snows that entrapped the party that fatal winter.

THE PIONEER MONUMENT
AT DONNER LAKE

The pioneer monument at Donner Lake was dedicated on June 6, 1918. The statue's base is as high as the snow that trapped the Donner Party (twenty-two feet). Present for the ceremony were (from left): Nevada governor Emmet D. Boyle, Patty Reed Lewis, Eliza Donner Houghton, Frances Donner Wilder, and California governor William D. Stephens. The attendees—including Virginia Reed Murphy—buried a time capsule that will be opened on June 6, 2018. (*The Bancroft Library*)

The gold is still plenty, plenty, plenty, and will continue plenty through this century and the next and the next! I truly wish you had left Springfield for California in '46 or '47. Independent of profits of mining operations, real estate has risen immensely. As for myself, I have a share, and a fair share, too, after all my misfortunes.

—James Reed, in a letter written on September 27, 1849, to a brother-in-law in Illinois

CHAPTER 10

The Survivors

The Donner Party survivors created good lives for themselves in California. Generally, they got what they came for—land, opportunity, and prosperity—which seemed to make their sufferings worthwhile. The disaster always shadowed them; it made them famous, or notorious, insofar as fame existed before mass media. But it didn't rule their lives.

For practical reasons, and possibly emotional ones, most survivors who weren't related didn't keep in touch. As on the trail, each family had its own life to live. And life was radically changing around them, from agricultural to industrial. In the mid-nineteenth century, people traveled on foot or by horse and carriage; lit their homes by candle or oil lamp; and generally lived by farming, mining, or developing land. During Virginia Reed's lifetime came the inventions that would shrink distances and speed up time: railroads, electricity, telephones, cars, airplanes, radio, and even an experiment called television.

Here is a brief look at what happened to key individuals and families:

Louis Keseberg

Was Keseberg truly evil, as so many accounts depict him? Or was he the Donner Party's scapegoat, as his defenders contend, singled out for blame because he was an outspoken foreigner from Prussia (now part of Germany)?

William Fallon, Ned Coffeemeyer, and others who rescued Keseberg thought he was a murderer. They spread the word that Keseberg had killed Tamsen Donner. Keseberg sued Coffeemeyer, charging defamation of character. (This was not the only tarnished view of the rescuers, some of whom were accused of robbing the people they were saving.)

Keseberg won, but his victory was hollow. The judge—none other than Captain John Sutter, owner of Sutter's Fort—awarded him token damages of one dollar.

While Keseberg denied it, many people claimed that he bragged about cannibalism and even called human liver his favorite meat. After working

Louis Keseberg's Lady Adams Hotel and Restaurant burned down, but the nearby Lady Adams Company building survived the fire of 1852 and is now the oldest building in Old Sacramento. *(Marian Calabro)*

briefly for Sutter, Keseberg ran a restaurant and hotel in Sacramento, called the Lady Adams. A local sheriff sarcastically commented: "I would like to board there, [but] I wouldn't!"

Where Keseberg went, disaster followed. His hotel did well during the gold rush, then burned down. Later he owned a brewery that was destroyed by a flood. His violent temper persisted; legal records show that he was twice brought to trial in California for assault.

After the death of their two babies in the snows, Keseberg and his wife, Philippine, went on to have eight more children. Two were severely brain damaged. To care for them, and to escape the taunts of "murderer" and "man-eater" that still clung to him, Keseberg retreated from society. Always anxious to clear his name, he took comfort when Eliza Donner Houghton publicly absolved him of any role in the death of her mother, Tamsen. Keseberg died at an old age.

The Murphys

Like Virginia Reed, teenager Mary Murphy wrote a long letter to her relatives back home shortly after reaching California. But Mary's outlook was not as hopeful as Virginia's. Mary lost six family members in the snows, including her mother, the widowed Levinah.

"I have nothing to live for, a poor orphan, Motherless and almost Friendless," Mary wrote. "I hope I shall not live long for I am tired of this troublesome world."

In fact, Mary was married within a month after her rescue. Women were in short supply in California; one male emigrant described it as "the finest country in the world! Women is all that is needed!"

The co-owner of Johnson's Ranch took Mary as his bride. She probably had little choice in the matter, being only about fifteen years old and having no adult family left to live with. Her husband abused her, but Mary's courage eventually returned: she managed to get a divorce—which was very difficult in the 1850s—and had a happier marriage to Charles Covillaud, who named the city of Marysville, California, for her. Her brother, William Murphy, became the city's attorney.

Mary Murphy Covillaud and two of her five children, Mary Ellen and Naomi *(California State Parks, Sutter's Fort State Historical Park)*

William Foster

William Foster was not tried for the deaths of Luis and Salvador, because killing Native Americans was not regarded as murder. He and his wife, Sarah, settled in California along the Yuba River, where the village of Foster's Bar is named for him. After losing their young son in the snows, they raised a new family. Foster also owned property in Marysville, the city named for his sister-in-law.

William Eddy

The man who led the Forlorn Hope out of its nightmare ended his journey with nothing. His wife and children were dead, his goods destroyed. Yet Eddy made a new life for himself in Gilroy, remarrying twice and living eleven years after rescue to enjoy his second family.

Eddy had vowed to murder Louis Keseberg for supposedly cannibalizing his son. It is said that in California he set out to make good on the threat but that James Reed and Edwin Bryant stopped him.

Eddy's memories of the Donner Party appeared in a popular book by Jessy Quinn Thornton, *Oregon and California in 1848,* in which Eddy portrayed himself as a hero. Some survivors and historians have agreed with Eddy's self-assessment. Others have called him a selfish liar. As with most aspects of Donner Party history, the truth is probably somewhere in between the two.

The Graveses

Elizabeth Graves, who drove such hard bargains with Margaret Reed over the ox hides on their roof, died during rescue. Her husband, Franklin, died in the Forlorn Hope. Six of their eight children lived. Mary Ann Graves, who survived the Forlorn Hope, became one of the first teachers in San Jose. Her brother William traveled east and lectured on the Donner Party. Supposedly

Unlike some other survivors, William Graves openly spoke about his Donner Party experiences. He was a teenager during the journey and carried a life-long hatred for James Reed, whom he considered arrogant and pretentious. *(California State Parks, Sutter's Fort State Historical Park)*

he said that the group's troubles began early; their entrapment, in his view, was a punishment from God for leaving Mr. Hardcoop to die.

Nancy Graves, who was about nine years old that winter, was left with unbearable memories. Not only did Nancy witness the painful decline of her mother and other family members, but apparently she was somehow tricked or confused into eating her mother's flesh. The orphaned girl could not recover, as one schoolmate described:

> I never recall my first schooldays in San Jose, without thinking of poor little Nancy G., who used to cry so much in school. Why that poor child used to break right out during schooltime, and it often seemed to me her heart would break. . . .
>
> One day my sister and two or three others gathered around her; we cried with her; and begged her to tell us what troubled her so much; and between sobs and sighs she told us of her being at "Starved Camp"—how her mother died, how part of her flesh was prepared for food without her knowledge. . . .
>
> We tried to soothe and comfort her but it seemed no use; for she would cry, "How can I forget it; or forgive myself?"

Nancy's outburst was unusual. This was a time when people kept their private sufferings and torments to themselves. More than one hundred years later, responses like Nancy's would be termed post-traumatic shock syndrome.

Hers was a classic case. Like many torture victims and prisoners of war, Nancy Graves was haunted throughout life by the horrors she experienced. Thirty years later she was a happily married mother of five, but still she told an interviewer that her memories would always be too painful to discuss. Other survivors may have felt what Nancy felt, to some degree, but they hid their feelings in public.

Why do some survivors of tragedies suffer for life, like Nancy Graves, while others such as Virginia Reed emerge without lasting emotional scars? Emmy Werner, a psychologist, is interested in the subject of children and survival. She has studied the young people of the Donner Party and has interviewed contemporary children living under the stress of war, chronic poverty, and physical disabilities.

Werner cites four survival characteristics or "roots of resilence." Successful survivors almost always enjoy affection from an extended family. They take on important responsibilities, which boosts their self-confidence. And they often have a special talent or skill, which they are encouraged to practice.

Finally, child survivors never lose hope, despite the odds. Some sort of faith, in a formal religion or otherwise, convinces them that things will work out. Their belief helps them transcend their current pain.

These factors certainly apply to the Breens, Reeds, and Donners, all of whom thrived in California.

The Breens

Patrick and Margaret Breen set down roots in San Juan Bautista, a town that had been settled by Spanish missionaries. There they farmed and had another child. Reaching California before the gold rush was a stroke of luck for their oldest son, John, the teenager whose special skill at Truckee Lake had been to bury the dead.

One of the first on the scene to pan for gold, John Breen amassed a fortune. His life's work was to run a ranch near his parents' farm; his business partner was his brother Edward, who as a boy had almost had his leg amputated on the journey west. John and Edward were renowned as honest and generous men. Eventually, after marrying and raising a large family, John Breen wrote his memoirs.

Their sister, Isabella, had been an infant at Truckee Lake. She gained fame as the last remaining survivor of the Donner Party, dying at age ninety, just a few years before World War II began. "I suppose I had the smallest chance of them all to survive, and now I am the last to be living," she told an interviewer. "How strange it seems to me!"

The Donners

Although all of the Donner children were orphaned, they found good homes. James and Margaret Reed adopted George's daughter Frances and Jacob's

The entire Breen family. Clockwise from top: William, James, Patrick Jr., John, Patrick Sr., Edward, Simon, and Peter. In the center are Isabella (top) and Margaret. *(California State Parks, Sutter's Fort State Historical Park)*

daughter Mary. Frances's younger sisters, Georgia and Eliza, were raised by a Swiss couple who lived near Sutter's Fort. The remaining children were absorbed into the families of teenagers Leanna and Elitha Donner, who married young.

The Donner survivors had long and productive lives, except Mary, who died giving birth to her first child.

Eliza Donner's life was interesting. Her husband, Sherman O. Houghton, was a U.S. senator from California, and Eliza appointed herself a sort of ambassador to the world for the Donner Party. She wrote a book about the group's experiences, although she had been a mere three-year-old playing with sunbeams that fateful winter. Some of her sisters and cousins were angry with her for publishing *The Expedition of the Donner Party and Its Tragic Fate,* because they preferred not to stir up painful memories.

Eliza Poor Donner Houghton, author of *The Expedition of the Donner Party and Its Tragic Fate*
(Author's collection)

The Reeds

Near skeletons when rescued, Margaret and the children recovered fast. "We are all verry fleshey," Virginia wrote in her letter to Mary. "Ma waies 10040 pon and still a gain[in]g. [Virginia, who had little practice writing numbers, meant 140 pounds.] I weight 81."

The Reeds settled in San Jose, a small town south of San Francisco founded by Spanish missionaries in 1777. (It is now one of California's largest cities.) There James Reed made the fortune he sought, thanks to the gold rush and real-estate speculation. He developed many of San Jose's streets and named them for his family: Margaret, Virginia, Martha, Keyes, and Reed.

Active in civic affairs, Reed was considered a model citizen and even served briefly as a sheriff and San Jose's chief of police. No one held the murder of John Snyder against him; it was seen as one of those unfortunate incidents that happened on the trail.

Like her husband, Margaret Reed thrived in California. "Margaret is fat and hearty, being healthy since she arrived, not even the sick headache[s],"

Virginia Street in San Jose, California, named by James Reed *(Marian Calabro)*

James reported to a relative in Illinois. The Donner adoptees added two seven-year-olds to the family, and the Reeds had two more children of their own: Charles, born nine months after his mother's rescue, and Willianoski, who died from a childhood disease.

The Reeds had a fine home and servants, just as in Springfield, and they entertained lavishly. According to a county historian: "The Reed home was

The Reeds at their home on Third and Margaret Streets in San Jose, probably around 1853.

This daguerreotype was never properly captioned, so some identities are in question. The young woman third from the right is probably Mary Donner or Frances Donner; both were orphans who were raised by the Reeds. The young woman second from the right may be Virginia Reed Murphy.

Left to right: James Reed; Charles Reed, born in California; Patty Reed; a toddler (barely visible), probably Willianoski Reed, also born in California; James Reed Jr.; Thomas Reed; another unidentified toddler (also barely visible), possibly Mary Murphy, Virginia's first child; and, at far right, Margaret Reed. *(California State Parks, Sutter's Fort State Historical Park)* always the scene of social gatherings, and at one of their large dinner parties it is said Mrs. Reed paid $16 apiece for turkeys and bought all that were to be had." (Sixteen dollars then was like one hundred dollars today.)

James Jr., who had trudged over the mountains as a six-year-old, did get his own horse. And as his rescuers predicted, the boy rode it everywhere. Even as an adult he rarely went anywhere on foot. James and his brothers, Thomas and Charles, became businessmen.

Virginia kept the vow she made to God on her darkest night during the ordeal: She became a Roman Catholic. She might also be called a convert to California, taking instantly to the rolling terrain that was so different from the flatness of the Midwest. As she wrote in her letter to Mary, "it is mostley in vallies . . . it is the greatest place for cattel and horses you ever saw . . . the spanards and Indians are the best riders i ever saw."

Thomas Reed in 1915
(California State Library)

Other things were catching her eye as well. Virginia urged her cousin to tell every Springfield girl "who wants to get Married to come to Callifornia." She eagerly reported that Eliza Williams, the family's deaf maid, now weighed 172 pounds and was about to be married.

Although Virginia didn't tell Mary, she had already gotten a marriage proposal. It came within a month of being rescued, while she was riding a mule at Johnson's Ranch. A young man rode beside her for a day, chatted in a friendly way, then popped the question. "I laugh even to this day when I think of it," Virginia said later. "I commenced laughing and said, 'I am going back to Springfield to go to school three or four years before I marry anyone.'" Her suitor ended up marrying the orphaned Elitha Donner instead.

Virginia never returned to Illinois. She was barely seventeen when she eloped with John M. Murphy, a U.S. Army officer who became a gold-rush millionaire and a real-estate tycoon like her father. He was not related to the Murphys of the Donner Party but had emigrated from the Midwest a few years earlier. By coincidence, he had helped build the cabin used by the Reeds and Breens at Truckee Lake.

James Reed disapproved of Virginia's conversion and Roman Catholic wedding, but he softened when his first grandchild arrived. Virginia had nine children in all, six of whom lived to adulthood. She kept up her horseback riding ("a horse has always been my pet of pets") and competed at county fairs; one observer called her "a handsome young lady, noted for her superior equestrianship."

Virginia helped run her husband's real-estate and insurance business and took it over when he died. She became the first woman on the West Coast to sell fire insurance. Throughout her life she never dropped the maiden name of which she was so proud; her signature was a firm *Virginia Reed Murphy*. Until a few years before her death she lived in San Jose.

Patty Reed, who married at eighteen and had nine children, also stayed nearby. Her marriage to Frank Lewis took place on Christmas 1856, ten years after Margaret had surprised her hungry children with their holiday meal at Truckee Lake. An article at the time said that the celebration included a "feast prepared by a company of Indians and native Spanish," with a side of beef roasted over a barbecue pit. Probably the wedding menu did not include the beans, rice, tripe, bacon, and dried apples that had seemed so magical when the family was starving.

At age fifty-seven, Virginia wrote a short memoir of the Donner Party that was published in *Century Magazine* and later as a book. An early draft of the article suggests that an editor rewrote much of Virginia's prose to make it easier to read. Her personality shines through in her original draft, in passages such as this: "I sometimes imagine I must be 1,000 years old now, it does not seem to me that I ever was a Child, and yet in many respects I am a Child even now."

Virginia Reed Murphy died peacefully at age eighty-seven. She never lost the spirit of the girl she had been, the twelve-year-old able to ride her own horse to the West and eager for the journey to begin.

Virginia Reed Murphy
(California State Library)

*They dined on ribs, and they laughed about it . . . as the
150th anniversary [of the Donner Party entrapment] draws near,
the families are proudly celebrating the survivors' role
in California history.*

—from a Knight-Ridder syndicated newspaper article by Kim Boatman, July 25, 1996

CHAPTER 11

The Donner Party Legacy

Ever since the winter of 1846–47, survivors and descendants of the Donner Party have struggled to show the world that cannibalism was only a small part of their story. One of their strongest supporters was the journalist who wrote their first book-length history. He was Charles Fayette McGlashan, editor of the *Truckee Republican* newspaper in Truckee, California, the town that grew up at the foot of Donner Pass.

McGlashan tracked down the survivors and interviewed almost all of them, in person or by letter. His timing was excellent. More than thirty years had passed since the disaster. After decades of keeping their guard up, his subjects seemed ready and even eager to reminisce. They were curious to learn what had happened to the others, and many who were orphaned, particularly as very young children, were anxious to learn more about their parents.

Some survivors, including Virginia Reed Murphy and Patty Reed Lewis, traded letters with McGlashan on and off for the rest of their lives. Clearly his questions set them thinking. "I remember many things distinctly," Virginia wrote to McGlashan. "I think it would have been better if my memory had

Charles McGlashan. His history of the Donner party, published in 1879 and still in print, was the first to emphasize fact over distortion. "The scenes of horror and despair ... need no exaggeration, no embellishment," he wrote. "The truth is sufficiently terrible." *(The Bancroft Library)*

been drug[g]ed." Louis Keseberg seized the opportunity to tell his side of the story.

Georgia Donner Babcock also welcomed McGlashan's efforts. " The veil should be removed from the past," she wrote. "[We] feel we are speaking to a world in which we have found many friends. . . . We show our appreciation by giving them the truest history the world will ever have of what took place at Donner Lake."

"More thrilling than romance, more terrible than fiction," trumpeted McGlashan's *History of the Donner Party: A Tragedy of the Sierra,* first published in 1879. The book was snapped up by readers all over the United States, sold well for decades, and is still in print.

Despite Georgia Donner's wish, McGlashan's account is not "the truest history." Interviewees sometimes altered facts to suit themselves. Others gave

Terrible! Thrilling! True!

HISTORY OF THE DONNER PARTY
A TRAGEDY OF THE SIERRA.

Price, Paper. - - $1.00.

Sent Prepaid to any Address on Receipt of Price,
By the Author, C. F. McGLASHAN, Truckee, Cal.

An advertisement for McGlashan's book *(Author's collection)*

information about parts of the trip they themselves hadn't made. For example, William Graves, whose family joined the Donner Party in August, reported on what had happened within the group from April through July.

And, unlike contemporary journalists, McGlashan gladly omitted or toned down sensitive details: "If possible, I would soften the accounts received from the other sources on account of the feelings of the children," even though those children had long been adults. He also tinkered with each new edition as he got more letters and changes from survivors. As a result, his *History of the Donner Party* is not consistent or fully objective.

Still, McGlashan's work is invaluable. It counteracted the overblown reports that had appeared for years in *The California Star* and other newspapers, and it became a starting point for other historians. McGlashan captured the voices of the survivors as no one else had. His book may have made them feel, at last, like heroes.

⟨⟨⟩⟩

The survivors certainly would have felt like heroes in 1996, as people celebrated the 150th anniversary of the start of the Donner Party journey.

Descendants of George and Jacob Donner gathered on the shores of Donner Lake. It wasn't the first Donner family reunion, but it was the biggest, drawing 450 people from as far away as Hawaii and Maryland. Most had never met each other. "My sister and I began by writing to 20 relatives and asking them to spread the word," said organizer Barbara Wilder Politano, a great-granddaughter of Frances Donner Wilder. "If we had imagined such a large event, we might have been afraid to start."

The weekend reunion left everyone feeling elated to be Donners, especially those who grew up ashamed or silent about their heritage. The oldest attendee, ninety-three-year-old Mary App Murray, a granddaughter of Leanna Donner App, recalled Leanna threatening to disown her if she ever read a history of the Donner Party. Even recently, the Donner connection was a stigma. "As a kid, it was never a positive," said Ann Donner Simon, a descendant of Jacob Donner. "Kids used to say, 'Don't sit next to Ann, she'll eat your arm off.'"

At California Trail Days in 1996, thousands of people gathered to celebrate the 150th anniversary of the Donner Party. *(Courtesy of Frankye Craig)*

Today, more than twenty-five hundred people have identified themselves as descendants of all the Donner Party members. They easily laugh off taunts about cannibalism and speak with pride of their ancestors' courage. Several hundred offspring from every family in the Donner Party—as well as kin of John Sutter, Charles McGlashan, and many of the teamsters and rescuers—made a pilgrimage to Donner Lake in August 1996 for California Trail Days, a weekend of historical festivities. Some even arrived by covered wagon.

It was a theatrical and intense event. Actors presented one-person shows, portraying such figures as Margaret Breen and Lansford Hastings. There was a mock inquest to probe the allegations against Louis Keseberg. (He was found not guilty of killing Tamsen Donner.) Someone cooked a kettle of Margaret Reed's Christmas soup.

For many who attended, it was as if the calendar had been turned back 150 years. Reporter and historian Frank Mullen Jr. calls the phenomenon "becoming unstuck in time" and says it is common among Donner Party devotees.

One of Mullen's favorite examples happened during Trail Days. After a one-man show on James Reed, a descendant of the Graves family laced into the actor *playing* Reed for murdering John Snyder. Carrying the Reed-Graves feud into the present, he also reprimanded James Frazier Reed III, an elderly descendent of the original Reed, who was in the audience. His parting shot to both men was: "And your two daughters are spoiled rotten!"

"He was apparently speaking of Virginia and Patty Reed, in their graves for more than 75 years," Mullen noted. "He was unstuck in time."

Emotions run high among the descendants, who recall poignant memories. One of the few things that brought a smile to Leanna Donner App's face was to ride in a car with the fresh air on her face; her stepsister Frances Donner Wilder always carried candy and snacks in her pockets and anxiously offered them to everyone around her. Joseph Cullumber, a great-great-grandson of Patrick and Margaret Breen, hates winter. "We have a place in the Sierra but I don't go up there in winter," he has said. "I don't like the snow. I don't know why; I just don't like the snow."

Donner Party descendants are realistic about their forebears. "My attitude is that they did what they did to survive and I wouldn't be here if they didn't," said Adam Breen, a college student. "I've heard all the bad jokes about finger foods and all that . . . when the world knows your family resorted to cannibalism to save themselves in the face of death, you'd better be able to laugh about it."

"I'm enormously proud of all my ancestors," declared Shirley McFarland, a direct descendant of Levinah Murphy and William Foster, who killed Luis and Salvador. "I don't care what they say about William. I feel he was a hero; he walked the snowline five times with two relief parties. He had to have been a fine person to put himself out like that. Levinah was, too—she cared for all the children, her own and others', throughout the ordeal."

Echoing the survivors themselves, James Frazier Reed III is past the point of assigning blame. In the saga of the Donner Party, he said, "there are enough errors to go around and there's enough heroism to go around."

Shirley McFarland and her granddaughter Elizabeth Marquez, descendants of Levinah Murphy and William and Sarah Foster, at the Emigrant Trail Museum in Donner Memorial State Park *(Marian Calabro)*

Could the Donner Party ordeal have ended differently? Could something like it happen again?

The most obvious reply to the first question is that the party might have avoided disaster by not taking the Hastings Cutoff. But they had sensible reasons for trying it. Lansford Hastings wasn't totally ignorant of the sierra, having crossed three times. And he himself took the shortcut just ahead of the Donner Party and made it safely to California with dozens of emigrants in wagons.

In fact, no one in the Donner Party held Hastings totally accountable for their troubles (although Virginia told McGlashan that taking the shortcut was "our fatal mistake"). Mostly they blamed the weather and themselves, especially their lack of leadership. "Our misfortunes were the result of bad management," James Reed declared a few months after the rescue. "Had I remained with the company, I would have had the whole of them over the mountains before the snow would have caught them; and those who have got through have admitted this to be true."

Not everyone saw the supremely self-confident Reed as their lost savior. "Reed was an intelligent and energetic man, and if he had remained the party might have got through," John Breen later mused. William Graves, however, always blamed the "aristocrat" Reed for the group's woes. "Oh I get mad every time I think of it," Graves told Charles McGlashan.

And if Hastings had to justify himself, he could have simply pointed to page 147 of his guide and asked why his accusers didn't follow this advice: "Emigrants should, invariably, arrive at Independence, Missouri, on or before the 15th day of April, so as to be in readiness to enter upon the journey." On April 15, the Reeds and Donners were just leaving home in Illinois.

In hindsight, some critics say that the party's biggest mistake was to hack their way across the thickly forested Wasatch Mountains rather than follow Weber Canyon. However, both routes were treacherous and might have slowed them down equally. The group even sent scouts ahead, including James Reed, before following what seemed to be the safer course.

It's also easy to fault the Donner Party for resting so many days along the trail—and for remaining one night too many at the summit. Again, however, these decisions were not made lightly. They seemed the right choices at the time and under the circumstances, which were far harsher than today's travelers could probably tolerate.

It is worth noting that no one in the Donner Party committed suicide (although Louis Keseberg considered it). Even in the depths of cold and starvation they were willing to live, literally, with their decisions.

George R. Stewart, author of a major history of the Donner Party, put the disaster into human perspective. "The story is basically one of people under stress," he said. That is why "it speaks to us still."

If we had been there, would we have killed the Native Americans for food, as William Foster did, or protested their murder, as William Eddy did?

Torn between staying with our spouse or our children, as Tamsen Donner was, what choice would we have made?

Would we emerge from the ordeal strong and happy, like Virginia Reed, or strong and tortured, like Nancy Graves?

Three of the strongest survivors: Virginia Reed Murphy, Patty Reed Lewis, and Frances Donner Wilder, 1918 *(The Bancroft Library)*

Severe stress is a psychological litmus test. It reveals the best and worst in people. Sometimes the Donner Party did act unpredictably—or took no action at all. But they were in the grip of forces they could not control. From the comfort of the twentieth century, it is easy to forget that they were lost and hungry even before they reached California, then they froze and starved for months.

The Donner Party still speaks to us, in part, *because* of their mistakes, their bad luck—and their grace. Certainly none of the survivors could forget their tragedies, but few dwelled on them. As best they could, they forgave themselves and made their peace with the world.

⚬⚬⚬

At first glance, it seems impossible that a Donner Party–like disaster could occur now. How could so many people be trapped for so long, in such an inaccessible place? Who could venture beyond the reach of telephones, two-way radios, global positioning systems, or rescue helicopters?

Yet a similar disaster did happen, including cannibalism, when a small airplane crashed into a remote mountain peak. The place was South America. The mountains were the Andes, which were blanketed in snow drifts up to one hundred feet deep. The forty people involved were traveling to a rugby tournament. The date was Friday, the thirteenth of October, 1972. This saga, made famous by Piers Paul Read in his book *Alive: The Story of the Andes Survivors,* shows that nature can still conquer technology.

The Andes party was like the Donner Party in many ways. Both groups consisted mainly of family members and friends, although a major difference is that no small children and few women were present among the South Americans. Both had state-of-the-art transportation that was no match for natural forces, whether it was the Pioneer Palace Car or a plane chartered from the Uruguay Air Force. Both tried to cross a dangerous mountain range during the worst winter in years, facing weather so bad that they waited for a day before making their crucial ascent.

And, once stranded, both groups were hard to reach despite the heroic attempts of rescue teams. When their food ran out, both groups searched desperately for other edibles until they resorted to eating the flesh of their dead.

Patty Reed Lewis, age eighty, on the ground that was the Truckee Lake encampment
(The Bancroft Library)

Eventually, both groups were rescued. Some survivors were shamed by their cannibalism and denied having done it. Work and faith helped them recover. Eventually, most people understood what the members of the Andes party and the Donner Party had endured and embraced them as heroes.

◦◦◦

The story of the Donner Party will never die. It lives on in a stream of non-fiction books, a video documentary, novels, plays, poems, interpretive dances, and even a fictionalized TV movie, *One More Mountain*.

The saga is particularly American. It says so much about the essence of the United States—about our restless spirit and hunger for land, our class and race divisions, our violence, our strength, our nerve. It reminds us that frontiers and obstacles come in all varieties and that the will to survive is our most primal instinct.

Virginia Reed understood the dark and bright sides of the journey. She came down on the side of optimism.

"O Mary I have not rote you half of the truble we have had but I have rote you anuf to let you now that you dont now what truble is," she wrote in her letter to her cousin.

She quickly added her final advice, "but Dont let this letter dishaten [dis-hearten] anybody   never take no cutofs and hury along as fast as you can."

VIRGINIA REED'S LETTER

⟨⟨⟨⟩⟩⟩

*Virginia was writing to her cousin, Mary Keyes,
in Springfield, Illinois.
Her original spelling and punctuation,
or lack thereof, are unchanged.*

Napa Vallie
California
May 16th 1847

My Dear Cousin   May the 16th 1847

    I take this oppertunity to write to you to let you now that we are all Well at present and hope this letter may find you all well to   My Dear Cousin I am going to write to you about our trubels geting to Callifornia. We had good luck til we come to big Sandy   thare we lost our best yoak of oxens we come to Brigers Fort & we lost another ox   we sold some of our provisions & baut a yoak of Cows & oxen and thay pursuaded us to take Hastings cutof over the salt plain   thay said it save 3 Hundred miles.   we went that road & we had to go through a long drive of 40 miles With out water Hastings said it was 40 but i think 80 miles   We traveld a day and night & a nother day and at noon pa went on to see if he coud find Water. he had not bin gone long till some of the oxen give out and we had to leve the wagons

and take the oxen on to water   one of the men staid with us and the others went on with the cattel to water   pa was a coming back to us with water
and met the men & thay was about 10 miles from water   pa said thay get to
water that nite and the next day to bring the cattel back for the wagons and
bring some water   pa got to us about noon   the man that was with us took
the horse and went on to water   We wated thare [hoping] he [would] come
we wated till night and We thought we [would] start and walk to Mr Donners
wagons that night   we took what little water we had and some bread and
started   pa caried Thomos and all the rest of us walk   we got to Donner and
thay were all a sleep so we laid down on the ground   we spred one shawl
down   we laid down on it and spred another over us and then put the dogs
on top   it was the couldes night you most ever saw   the wind blew and if
it haden bin for the dogs we would have Frosen   as soon as it was day we
went to Mrs Donners she said we could not walk to the Water and if we staid
we could ride in thare wagons to the spring   so pa went on to the water to
see why thay did not bring the cattel   when he got thare thare was but one
ox and cow thare   none of the rest had got to water   Mr. Donner come
out that night with his cattel and brought his wagons and all of us in   we
staid thare a week and Hunted for our cattel and could not find them   so
some of the compania took thare oxens and went out and brout in one
wagon and cashed the other tow [two] and a grate many things all but What
we could put in one wagon   we Had to devied our provisions out to them
to get them to carie it   We got three yoak with our ox & cow   so we went
on that way a while and we got out of provisions and pa had to go on to
Callifornia for provisions   we could not get along that way.   in 2 or 3 days
after pa left we had to cash our wagon and take Mr graves wagon and cash
some more of our things. well we went on that way a while and then we had
to get Mr eddies wagon   we went on that way a while and then we had to
cash all our close except a change or 2 and put them in Mr Bri [Breen's]
Wagon and Thomos & James rode the other 2 horses and the rest of us had
to walk.   we went on that way a While and we come to a nother long drive
of 40 miles and then we went with Mr Donner We had to walk all the time
we was a travling up the truckee river   we met a man [Charles Stanton] and

to [two] Indians that we had sent on for provisions to Suter Fort   thay had
met pa not fur from Suters Fort   he looked very bad   he had not ate but 3
times in 7 days and the three last days without any thing   his horse was not
abel to carrie him   thay give him a horse and he went on   so we cashed
some more of our things all but what we could pack on one mule and we
started   Martha and James road behind the two Indians   it was a raing [rain-
ing] then in the Vallies and snowing on the montains so we went on that way
3 or 4 days till we come to the big mountain or the Callifornia Mountain
the snow then was about 3 feet deep thare was some wagons thare   thay said
thay had atempted to croos and could not. well we thought we would try it
so we started and thay started again with those wagons   the snow was then
up to the mules side   the farther we went up the deeper the snow got so
the wagons could not go   so thay pack thare oxens and started with us carring a child a piece and driving the oxens in snow up to thare wast [waist]   the
mule Martha and the Indian was on was the best one   so thay went and broak
the road and that indian was the Pilet   so we wint on that way 2 miles and
the mules kept faling down in the snow head formost and the Indian said he
could not find the road   we stoped and let the Indian and man go on to hunt
the road thay went on and found the road to the top of the mountain and
come back and said thay thought we could git over if it did not snow any
more   well the Weman were all so tirder [tired] caring there Children that
thay could not go over that night so we made a fire and got something to
eat & ma spred down a bufalo robe & we all laid down on it & spred
somthing over us & ma sit up by the fire & it snowed one foot on top of the
bed   so we got up in the morning & the snow was so deep we could not
go over & we had to go back to the cabin & build more cabins & stay thar
all winter without Pa we had not the first thing to eat   Ma maid [made]
arrangements for some cattel giving 2 for 1 in callifornia we seldom thot of
bread for we had not any since I [could remember] & the cattel was so poor
thay could not git up when thay laid down   we stoped thare the 4th of
November & staid till March and what we had to eat i cant hardley tell you
& we had that man [Stanton] & Indians to feed to   well thay started over a
foot and had to come back   so thay made snowshoes and started again & it

come on a storm & thay had to come back it would snow 10 days before it would stop thay wated till it stoped and started again   I was a going with them & I took sick & could not go. thare was 15 started & thare was 7 got throw   5 weman & 2 men it come a storme and thay lost the road & got out of provisions & the ones that got throwe had to eat them that Died   not long after thay started we got out of provisions & had to put matha [Martha] at one cabin James at another Thomas at another & Ma and Elizia & Milt Eliot & I dried up what little meat we had and started to see if we could get across & had to leve the childrin   o Mary you may think that hard to leve theme [them] with strangers & did not now [know] whether we would see them again or not   we couldnt hardle get a way from them but we told theme we would bring them Bread & then thay was willing to stay   we went & was out 5 days in the mountains   Eliza giv out & had to go back we went on a day longer   we had to lay by a day & make snowshows [snowshoes] & we went on a while and coud not find the road so we had to turn back   I could go on verry well while i thout we were giting along but as soone as we had to turn back i could hadley get along but we got to the cabins that night & I froze one of my feet verry bad   that same night thare was the worst storme we had that winter & if we had not come back that night we would never got back   we had nothing to eat but ox hides   o Mary I would cry and wish I had what you all wasted   Eliza had to go to Mr. Graves cabin & we staid at Mr Breen thay had meat all the time. & we had to kill littel cash the dog & eat him   we ate his entrails and feet & hide & evry thing about him o my Dear Cousin you dont now what trubel is yet. Many a time we had on the last thing a cooking and did not now wher the next would come from but there was awl weis some way provided   there was 15 in the cabon we was in and half of us had to lay a bed all the time   thare was 10 starved to death then   we was hadly abel to walk   we lived on little cash a week and after Mr. Breen would cook his meat we would take the bones and boil them 3 or 4 days at a time   ma went down to the other cabin and got half a hide carried it in snow up to her wast   it snowed and would cover the cabin all over so we could not git out for 2 or 3 days   we would have to cut pieces of the logs in sied to make the fire with   I could hardly eat the hides and had not eat anything 3 days   Pa stated [started] out to us with provisions and then come a storm and he could not go   he cash his provision and went back on the other side of the bay to get a compana of men and the San Wakien [Joaquin] got so hye he could not cross   well thay Made up a Compana at Suters Fort and sent out   we had not ate anything for 3 days & we had onely half a hide and we was out on top of the cabin and we seen them a coming

O my Dear Cousin you dont now how glad i was   we run and met them one of them we knew   we had traveled with him on the road   thay staid there 3 days to recruit us a little so we could go   thare was 21 started   all of us started and went a piece and Martha and Thomas give out and the men had to take them back   Ma and Eliza & James and I come on and o Mary that was the hades [hardest] thing yet to come on and leiv them thar   did not now but what thay would starve to Death   Martha said well Ma if you never see me again do the best you can   the men said they could hadly stand it   it maid them all cry but they said it was better for all of us to go on for if we was to go back we would eat that much more from them   thay give them a little meat and flore [flour] and took them back and we come on   we went over great hye mountain as strait as stair steps in snow up to our knees   litle James walk the hole way over all the mountain in snow up to his waist.   he said every step he took he was a gitting nigher Pa and somthing to eat   the Bears took the provision the men had cashed and we had but very little to eat   when we had traveld 5 days travel we me [met] Pa with 13 men going to the cabins   o Mary you do not now how glad we was to see him   we had not seen him for 6 months   we thought we woul never see him again   he heard we was coming and he made some seet [sweet] cakes to give us   he said he would see Martha and Thomas the naxt day   he went in tow [two] days what took us 5 days   some of the compana was eating them that Died but Thomas & Martha had not ate any   Pa and the men started with 17 peaple Hiram G. Miller carried Thomas and Pa caried Martha and thay wer caught in [storms] and thay had to stop two days   it stormed so they could not go and the Bears took their provisions and thay were 4 days without any thing Pa and Hiram and all the men started   one Donner boy [sentence unfinished] Pa a carring Martha   Hiram caring Thomas and the snow was up to thare wast and it a snowing so thay could hadly see the way. thay raped [wrapped] the children up and never took them out for 4 days thay had nothing to eat in all that time Thomas asked for somthing to eat once   them that thay brought from the cabins some of them was not able to come and som would not come that was 3 died and the rest eat them thay was 11 days without any thing to eat but the Dead   Pa braught Tom and pady [Patty] on to where we was none of the men was abel to go there feet was froze very bad so thay was a nother Compana went and brought then all in thay are all in from the mauntains now but four thay was men went out after them and was caught in a storm and had to come back   thare was a nother compana gone thare was half got through that was stoped thare   thare was but [two] families that all of them got [through] we was one   O Mary I have not rote you half of the truble we have had but I have rote you anuf to let you now that you dont now what truble is   but thank god we have all got throw and the onely family that did not eat human flesh we have left everything but i dont cair for that we have got throw with our lives but Dont let this letter dishaten [dishearten] anybody never take no cutofs and hury along as fast as you can.

My Dear Cousin

We are all very well pleased with Callifornia particulary with the climate let it be ever so hot a day thare is allwais cool nights it is a beautiful Country it is mostley in vallies it aut to be a beautiful Country to pay us for our trubel giting there it is the greatest place for cattel and horses you ever saw   it would Just suit Charley for he could ride down 3 or 4 horses a day and he could lern to be Bocarro [vaquero] that one who lases [lassos] cattel the spanards and Indians are the best riders i ever saw they have a spanish sadel and woden sturups and great big spurs the wheels of them is 5 inches in diameter and they could not manage the Callifornia horses witout the spurs. thay wont go atol if thay cant hear the spurs rattle that have littel bells to them to make them rattle thay blindfold the horses and then sadel them and git on them and then take the blindfole of [off] and let [them] run and if thay cant sit on thay tie themselves on and let them run as fast as they can and go out to a band of bullluck and throw the reatter [riata] on a wild bullluck and put it around the horn of his sadel and he can hold it as long as he wants another Indian throwes his reatter on its feet and throw them and when thay take the reatter of [off] of them thay are very dangerous thay will run after them hook there horses and run after any person thay see thay ride from 80 to 100 miles a day some of the spanard have from 6 to 7000 head of horses and from 15 to 16000 head cattel we are all verry fleshey Ma waies 10040 pon [140 pounds] and still a gaing [gaining] I weight 81 tell Henriet if she wants to get Married to come to Callifornia she can get a spanyard any time. that Eliza is a going to mariye a spanyard by the name of Armeho [Armijo] and Eliza weigh 10072 We have not saw uncle Cadon yet but we have had 2 letters from him he is well and is a coming here as soon as he can Mary take this letter to uncle Gursham and to all that i know to all of our neighbors [and tell Dochter Maniel] and every girl i know and let them read it Mary kiss little Sue and Maryan for me and give my best love to all i know to uncle James aunt Lida and all the rest of the famila and to uncle Gursham and aunt Percilla and all the Children and to all of our neighbors and to all the girls i know Ma sends her very best love to uncle James aunt Lida and all the rest of the famila and to uncle Gursham and aunt Persilla all of the Children and to all of our neighbors and to all she knows. pa is [at] yerbayan [Yerba Buena] so no more at present

My Dear casons
Virginia Elizabeth B Reed

CHRONOLOGY

⟨❧⟩

Like every chronology of the Donner Party, this one is approximate. It is based mainly on Frank Mullen Jr.'s *The Donner Party Chronicles,* a day-by-day account. Mullen explains why it is impossible to pinpoint an accurate Donner Party time line: "Read sixty books involving the Donners and you'll get sixty variations. Simple matters, like when or where things happened or who they happened to, become debates. Mileages don't tally. Timetables do not compute."

1846

April 15	The Reed and Donner families and their hired hands leave Springfield, Illinois, for California
April–May	Travel through Illinois and Missouri
May 11	Arrive at Independence, Missouri
May 19	Travel in tandem with another emigrant wagon train, the Russell Party, for safety against Native Americans and warring Mexicans
May 29	Sarah Keyes, grandmother of Virginia Reed, dies in Kansas territory of chronic illness

June	Travel through Nebraska territory; hunt buffalo; more families join the wagon train
July 4	Celebrate Independence Day at La Prele Creek (Wyoming)
mid-July	Vote to take the Hastings Cutoff, a supposed shortcut; the Russell Party and other emigrants continue on the established route. George Donner elected captain; group becomes known as the Donner Party
July 26–30	Stop at Fort Bridger (Wyoming) for final provisions
July 31	Set out on the Hastings Cutoff (Utah)
August 6-11	Reach impassable Weber Canyon (Utah); group waits while three members seek guidance from Lansford Hastings, who recommended the shortcut and is ahead on the trail
mid-August	Cut a wagon road through the densely forested Wasatch Mountains (Utah)

The Graves-Fosdick group, a family from Illinois, joins the caravan. The Donner Party now numbers eighty-seven people: the Reeds; the Donners; the Breens, recent Irish immigrants from Iowa; the Eddys, from Illinois; the Graveses and Fosdicks; the Kesebergs, Wolfingers, and other German immigrants; the McCutchens, from Missouri; the Murphys, Fosters, and Pikes, an extended family from Missouri and Tennessee; and several friends and hired hands of the various families.

August 25	Luke Halloran, an invalid traveling with the Donners, dies of chronic illness
End of August	Reach the Great Salt Lake (Utah); rest
Early September	Cross the Great Salt Lake Desert (Utah); run out of water; lose many oxen; camp for several nights; Reeds and others abandon some wagons in order to move on

September 10	Low on food and supplies; Charles Stanton and William McCutchen ride ahead to Sutter's Fort in California for provisions
September 29	Rejoin the established route at the Humboldt River (Nevada)
October 5	James Reed is banished from the Donner Party for killing John Snyder, an employee of the Graves family; Reed rides ahead to Sutter's Fort for supplies
October 8–9	Margaret Reed is forced to abandon the family's last covered wagon; Mr. Hardcoop, traveling with the Kesebergs, is left to die
October 13–14	Cross the Forty-Mile Desert at the end of the Humboldt River; Mr. Wolfinger is killed under mysterious circumstances
mid-October	Rest for several days at Truckee Meadows (modern-day Reno, Nevada) before entering the Sierra Nevada
October 21	William Pike is killed when his pistol is accidentally discharged
Late October	Stanton and two Native Americans, Luis and Salvador, reach the Donner Party with supplies
	James Reed reaches Sutter's Fort; teams up with McCutchen, held behind by illness, to make rescue attempt
	First major snowfall in Sierra Nevada; snow and rain continue with few breaks through November 11
October 27–30	Most of Donner Party reaches Truckee Lake (now Donner Lake in California), near mountain summit; the Donner families are detained several miles behind by accident and injury

October 31–November 3	Donner Party makes several attempts but cannot cross summit, due to severe weather and fatigue
October 31	Snow stops rescuers Reed and McCutchen from crossing summit eastbound; they return to Sutter's Fort and Yerba Buena (San Francisco) to recruit more rescuers
November 4	Families slaughter oxen for food; set up camps for winter at Alder Creek and Truckee Lake; a total of eighty-one are entrapped
November 20	Patrick Breen begins diary
November 25–December 3	Second storm
Late November	Twenty-two people try and fail to cross summit; return to camps, where deaths begin
December 9–13	Third storm
December 16	Fifteen-member snowshoe party (Forlorn Hope) sets out in desperation for help
December 23–25	Fourth storm
December 25	Margaret Reed takes food out of hiding for family's Christmas dinner
December 25–27	First cannibalism takes place among the Forlorn Hope

1847

January 4–8	Margaret Reed, Virginia Reed, Milt Elliott, and Eliza Williams try and fail to cross summit; return to camp; Virginia's feet frozen; Reeds given shelter by Breens
January 9–13	Fifth storm

January 10	Luis and Salvador, part of the Forlorn Hope, killed by William Foster
mid-January	Native Americans guide Forlorn Hope survivors out of the mountains; William Eddy first to reach safety
January 22–27	Sixth storm
January 31	First rescue team, led by Aquilla Glover, leaves Sutter's Fort
February	Cannibalism among the entrapped; Reeds probably do not partake
February 2–6	Seventh storm
February 7	Second rescue team, led by James Reed, leaves Yerba Buena
February 18	First rescue team reaches Truckee Lake; departs February 22 with twenty-three people, including the Reeds, but Patty and Tommy must turn back
February 27	Margaret, Virginia, and Jimmy Reed reunited with James Reed in mountains
March 1	Second rescue team reaches Truckee Lake; departs March 3 with seventeen people
March 6–8	Eighth storm; second rescue team snowbound; some stay behind to be brought in by third rescue team
March 12	Third rescue team, led by William Foster and William Eddy, reaches Truckee Lake; departs March 13 with four people
March 20	Patrick Breen stops keeping his diary

February–March	Five die during rescue attempts; two die shortly after rescue
February–April	Forty-seven survivors reach California
March 28–April 3	Ninth storm
April 17	Fourth rescue party, led by William Fallon, reaches Truckee Lake; departs April 20 with Louis Keseberg, last person alive in the winter camps
Spring	Newspapers begin to print sensationalized accounts of the Donner Party
May 16	Virginia Reed writes a long letter about her recent experiences to her cousin in Springfield, Illinois
June 22	Truckee Lake camp is partly cleared and burned down by U.S. Army soldiers
Summer	Edwin Bryant, traveling east, carries Virginia's letter to Spring-field
December 16	Virginia's letter appears in the *Illinois Journal*

ROSTER OF THE DEAD

Exact dates of deaths are given, where known. Ages are approximate.

Six deaths along the trail, 1846

Luke Halloran (25), August 25, of illness

Mr. Hardcoop (60?), early October, ill and abandoned

Sarah Keyes (70?), May 29, of illness

William Pike (25?), October 20, accidental shooting

John Snyder (25?), October 5, killed by James Reed

Mr. Wolfinger (30?), early October, killed, possibly by Spitzer and Reinhardt

Twenty-two deaths in winter camp, 1846–47

Karl Burger (30?), December 29

Elizabeth Donner (45), March

George Donner (60?), March

Jacob Donner (56?), December

Lewis Donner (3), March

Samuel Donner (4), March

Tamsen Donner (44), March

Eleanor Eddy (25), February 7

James Eddy (3), March

Margaret Eddy (1), February 3

Milford (Milt) Elliott (28), February 9

George Foster (4), March

Louis Keseberg Jr. (1), December 24

Harriet McCutchen (1), February 2

John Murphy (15), January 3

Levinah Murphy (36), March

Catherine Pike (1), February 20

Joseph Reinhardt (30), December

Samuel Shoemaker (25?), December

James Smith (25?), December
Augustus Spitzer (30?), February 7
Baylis Williams (25?), December 14

Eight deaths in the snowshoe party (Forlorn Hope), 1846–47
Antonio (23?), December
Patrick Dolan (35?), December 25
Jay Fosdick (23), January
Franklin Graves (57), December 25
Lemuel Murphy (12), December
Charles Stanton (35), December 21
Luis (age unknown), January, killed by William Foster
Salvador (age unknown), January, killed by William Foster

Five deaths during rescue attempts, 1847
John Denton (28?), February
Isaac Donner (5), March
Elizabeth Graves (45), March
Franklin Graves Jr. (5), March
Ada Keseberg (3), February

Two deaths shortly after rescue, 1847
Elizabeth Graves (1), March
William Hook (12), February 28, while overeating

FOR FURTHER RESEARCH

渻

BOOKS FOR YOUNG READERS

Freedman, Russell. *Children of the Wild West.* New York: Clarion Books, 1983. Photos and text depict the daily life of young people in the Old West. No references to the Donner Party, but a good overview of their times.

Laurgaard, Rachel. *Patty Reed's Doll.* Davis, California: Tomato Enterprises, 1981. For younger readers. This fictionalized look at the Donner Party, which does not mention cannibalism, tells the story from the viewpoint of Patty's doll. A teacher's guide is available, keyed to the fourth-grade level.

Lavender, David. *Snowbound: The Tragic Story of the Donner Party.* New York: Holiday House, 1996. A factual account, clear and concise, by an award-winning historian. Contains relatively few quotes from the writings and remembrances of Donner Party members.

Luchetti, Cathy, and Carol Olwell. *Women of the West.* New York: Orion Books, 1982. Contains profiles of eleven frontier women, including Sarah Winnemucca, told in their own words. Well-illustrated and particularly sensitive to the minority experience.

Murphy, Jim. *Across America on an Emigrant Train.* New York: Clarion Books, 1993. Follows a railroad journey to California made in 1879 by the writer Robert Louis Stevenson. Some of his trip paralleled the route taken by the Donner Party. Gives a good sense of how the West developed after the gold rush.

Philip, Neil, ed. *In a Sacred Manner I Live: Native American Wisdom.* New York: Clarion Books, 1997. This collection of speeches and excerpts by Native American leaders includes commentary on the devastation of their land and tribal life during the white migration westward.

Stefoff, Rebecca. *Women Pioneers.* New York: Facts On File, 1997. Virginia Reed is among the nine pioneer women profiled in this informative collection.

Werner, Emmy E. *Pioneer Children on the Journey West.* Boulder, Colorado: Westview Press, 1995. Scholarly yet readable, this fascinating book is based on the diaries, letters, and reminiscences of 120 children and teenagers who took part in the westward migration. Includes an excellent chapter on the young people of the Donner Party.

Wexler, Sanford. *Westward Expansion: An Eyewitness History.* New York: Facts On File, 1991. Rich in illustrations, chronologies, and quotes.

Zeinert, Karen, ed. *Across the Plains in the Donner Party.* North Haven, Connecticut: Linnet Books, 1996. A brief yet thoughtful and complete overview, told mainly through primary source materials such as Virginia Reed's 1847 letter, her 1891 magazine article, Patrick Breen's diary, and the letters of James Reed.

VIDEOS

The Donner Party. Written and directed by Ric Burns. Direct Cinema, Ltd., 1992.

The Donner Party. Part of the series *The Real West,* initially aired on the Arts & Entertainment Network. Greystone Productions, 1994.

On the Trail of the Tragedy. A documentary about the archaeological excavation of the Donner camp near Alder Creek. Available at Donner Memorial State Park, Truckee, California.

WEB SITES

Most of these sites contain maps and links to dozens of related sites.

http://www.kn.pacbell.com/wired/donner
Pacific Bell's "Donner Online" interactive site for students.

http://www.sfmuseum.org/hist6/donner.html
Donner Party holdings of the San Francisco History Museum.

http://www.metrogourmet.com/crossroads/KJhome.htm
A site founded by librarian and historian Kristin Johnson, entitled "New Light on the Donner Party."

http://sunsite.berkeley.edu/calheritage
A digital archive of California history collections from The Bancroft Library at the University of California, Berkeley.

BIBLIOGRAPHY

Baxter, Don J. *Gateways to California.* San Francisco: Pacific Gas and Electric Company, 1968.

Boatman, Kim. "Donners Lived to Dine on Ribs." New Orleans *Times-Picayune,* July 25, 1996, p. 14.

Breen, John. "Account of His Experiences with the Donner Party as Told to Mrs. Eliza W. Farnham." In *California In-Doors and Out.* New York: Dix, Edwards, 1856. Reprint, Nieuwkoop: B. de Graaf, 1972.

——. "Pioneer Memories." Manuscript C-D 51. University of California, Berkeley, Bancroft Library, 1877.

Brown, Dee. *The Gentle Tamers: Women of the Old West.* New York: G. P. Putnam's Sons, 1958.

Bryant, Edwin. *What I Saw in California: Being a Journal of a Tour by the Emigrant Route and South Pass.* New York: D. Appleton, 1848. Reprint, Lincoln: University of Nebraska Press, 1985.

Craig, Frankye, ed. *The Donner Party: An American Tragedy. 150th Anniversary Commemorative Update, Volume One.* Reno, Nevada: Events/By Design, 1997.

DeVoto, Bernard. *Year of Decision, 1946.* Boston: Houghton Mifflin, 1943.

Donner, Eliza. "Letters to C. F. McGlashan." Manuscript C-B 570. Box I, Folder 20. University of California, Berkeley, Bancroft Library, 1879.

Donner, Tamsen. "Letter of May 11, Written on the Trail to Her Sister from "Independence, Missouri." Manuscript. San Marino, California, Huntington Library, 1846. Reprinted in *Covered Wagon Women,* vol. I, edited by Kenneth L. Holmes, Glendale, California: Arthur H. Clark, 1983.

Freedman, Russell. *Children of the Wild West.* New York: Clarion Books, 1983.

Graves, Mary Ann. "Letter from California." *Illinois Gazette,* Lacon, Illinois, September 9, 1847.

Griffith, Martin. "Anniversary of Tragic Voyage." *San Francisco Chronicle,* July 20, 1996.

Hall, Carroll D., ed. *Donner Miscellany: 41 Diaries and Documents.* San Francisco: Book Club of California, 1947.

Hardesty, Donald L. *The Archaeology of the Donner Party.* Reno: University of Nevada Press, 1997.

Hastings, Lansford W. *Emigrants' Guide to Oregon and California.* Cincinnati: G. Concklin, 1845. Reprint, Bedford, Massachusetts: Applewood Books, 1994.

Hawkins, Bruce R., and David B. Madsen. *Excavation of the Donner-Reed Wagons: Historic Archaeology Along the Hastings Cutoff.* Salt Lake City: University of Utah Press, 1990.

Heizer, Robert F., and Albert B. Elsasser. *The Natural World of the California Indians.* Berkeley: University of California Press, 1980.

History of Santa Clara County, California. San Francisco: Alley, Bowen & Co., Publishers, 1881.

Holt, Daniel D. "Had I remained with the company . . ." *Overland Journal,* 1996, pp. 17-27.

Houghton, Eliza Poor Donner. *The Expedition of the Donner Party and Its Tragic Fate.* Chicago: A.C. McClurg, 1911.

Johnson, Kristin, ed. *"Unfortunate Emigrants": Narratives of the Donner Party.* Logan: Utah State University Press, 1996.

King, Joseph A. *Winter of Entrapment: A New Look at the Donner Party.* Toronto: P. D. Meany, 1992. Revised edition, Walnut Creek, California: K & K Books, 1994.

Korns, J. Roderic, compiler. *West from Fort Bridger: The Pioneering of Immigrant Trails Across Utah, 1846–1850.* Edited by Korns and Dale Morgan. Revised and updated by Will Bagley and Harold Schinkler. Logan: Utah State University Press, 1994.

Lewis, Donovan. *Pioneers of California.* San Francisco: Scottwall Associates, 1993.

Lewis, Oscar. *The Autobiography of the West.* New York: Henry Holt and Company, 1958.

Limerick, Patricia Nelson. *The Legacy of Conquest.* New York: Norton, 1987.

McFarland, Shirley. Interview by author. Donner Party family reunion, Reno, Nevada, September 27, 1997.

McGlashan, Charles Fayette. *History of the Donner Party: A Tragedy of the Sierra.* Truckee, California: *Truckee Republican,* 1880. Reprint, California: Stanford University Press, 1940.

McGlashan, M. Nona, and Betty H. McGlashan, eds. *From the Desk of Truckee's C. F. McGlashan.* Truckee, California: Truckee-Donner Historical Society, 1986.

McHugh, Thomas P. *Hazeldell Charivari. Christmas at Zayante: The Wedding of Patty Reed Lewis.* 1859. Reprint. Santa Cruz, California: *Frontier Gazette,* 1959.

Meschery, Joanne. *Truckee: An Illustrated History of the Town and Its Surroundings.* Truckee, California: Rocking Stone Press, 1978.

Morgan, Dale L., ed. *Overland in 1846: Diaries and Letters of the California-Oregon Trail.* 2 vols., 1963. Reprint, Lincoln: University of Nebraska Press, 1993.

Mullen, Frank, Jr. *The Donner Party Chronicles: A Day-by-Day Account of a Doomed Wagon Train 1846–1847.* Reno: Nevada Humanities Committee (Halcyon Imprint), 1997.

Murphy, Mary. "Three Letters Written to Dear Uncles, Aunts, and Cousins, May 25." Typescript. Covillaud Family Files. Marysville, California, Yuba County Library, 1847.

Neider, Charles, ed. *The Great West.* New York: Coward-McCann, 1958.

Reed, James Frazier. "Diary." Folder 85, Martha Reed Lewis Papers. Sacramento, California: Sutter's Fort Historical Museum, 1847.

——. "Letter to James Keyes." *Illinois State Register,* vol. XIV, no. 30, September 27, 1849.

Reed, Virginia. "Letter Written to Her Cousin, Mary C. Keyes, May 16." Manuscript 89/127C. University of California, Berkeley, Bancroft Library, 1847. Reprinted in *The Illinois Journal* (Springfield), December 16, 1847.

Reed, Virginia (Murphy). "Letters to C. F. McGlashan." Manuscript C-B 570. Box II, Folder 48. University of California, Berkeley, Bancroft Library, 1879.

——. "Letter to Garnett, May 17." University of California, Berkeley, Bancroft Library, 1912.

——. "Memoir: June 1879." Folder 100. University of California, Berkeley, Bancroft Library, 1879.

——. *Across the Plains in the Donner Party: A Personal Narrative of the Overland Trip to California, 1846-1847.* Special (July) edition of *Century Magazine,* 1891. Reprint, Golden, Colorado: Outbooks, 1980.

Rhoads, Daniel. "Relief of the Donner Party." Manuscript C-D 144. University of California, Berkeley, Bancroft Library, 1873.

Sawyer, Eugene T. *History of Santa Clara County.* Los Angeles: Historic Records Co., 1922.

Schlissel, Lillian. *Women's Diaries of the Westward Journey.* New York: Schocken Books, 1982.

Scott, John Anthony. *The Ballad of America: The History of the United States in Song and Story.* New York: Bantam Books, Inc., 1966.

Stefoff, Rebecca. *Women Pioneers.* New York: Facts On File, 1995.

Stewart, George R. *Ordeal by Hunger: The Story of the Donner Party* (Second Edition). Originally published 1936. Boston: Houghton Mifflin Company, 1960. Reprint, Lincoln: University of Nebraska Press, 1986.

Stone, Irving. *Men to Match My Mountains.* Garden City, New York: Doubleday, 1956.

Thornton, Jessy Quinn. *Oregon and California in 1848.* 2 vols. New York: Harper & Bros., 1849. Donner Party material reprinted as *Camp of Death.* Golden, Colorado: Outbooks, 1986.

Unruh, John D., Jr. *The Plains Across: The Overland Emigrants and the Trans-Mississippi West: 1840–1860.* Urbana: University of Illinois Press, 1979.

Werner, Emmy E. *Pioneer Children on the Journey West.* Boulder, Colorado: Westview Press, 1995.

Winnemucca, Sarah Hopkins. *Life Among the Piutes: Their Wrongs and Claims.* New York: G. P. Putnam Sons, 1883. Reprint, Reno: University of Nevada Press, 1994.

Zeinert, Karen, ed. *Across the Plains in the Donner Party.* North Haven, Connecticut: Shoe String Press, 1996.

INDEX

Page numbers in **bold** refer to illustrations.

Murphy, Virginia. *See* Reed, Virginia

Murphy, William (Billy), **90, 124,** 141

Murray, Mary App, 156

Native Americans, 18, 20, 23, 31, 33, 38–39, **38,** 52,
    59, 64, 69, 73, 75, 77, 82, 109, 111, 142, 182
  as guides. *See under* Donner Party
  and Sutter's Fort, 66, 78, 109, 129
  at Truckee Lake, 102–4
  and "Truckee" name, 79, 103

Nebraska, 34–35

Nevada, 65–66, **66,** 76, **76, 77,** 79, **80,** 138

Newspapers, 17, 18, 25, 131, **131,** 155

Oregon, 18–19, 27, 42–43, 66, 131–32, 143

Oregon Trail, 19, 42

Oxen, 17–18, 20, 25, 28, **28,** 32, 52, 69, 77, 80, 85,
    165–67
  as currency, 91
  and desert crossing, 59–63
  as food, 91, 94–96, 98, **99,** 100–101, 128, 168–69
  hides of, **90,** 91, 95–96, 98–101, **99,** 143, 168–69
  and Snyder's stabbing, 69

Pike, William (and Pike family), 41, 54, 56, 64, 81,
    90, 91–92

Pilot Peak, 63

Pioneer Palace Car. *See under* Covered wagons

Platte River, **11,** 35, 36

Politano, Barbara Wilder, 156

Polk, James K., **31**

Post-traumatic shock syndrome, 144

Prosser Reservoir, **94**

Ragtown, 78

Railroads, **53, 83,** 133–36, **133,** 182

Read, Piers Paul, 161

Reed, Charles, 149–50, **149**

Reed, James Frazier, 17–20, **21,** 24–26, 30, 32, 39,
    56, **126,** 129, 139, 143, **143, 149,** 151, 159. *See
    also* Reed family
  banishment of, 70–73, 126, 129
  and Black Hawk War, 18, 37

Reed, James Frazier *(cont.)*
  and buffalo hunting, 34–35, **35**
  and California Land, 18, 111
  designs Pioneer Palace Car, 21
  and Hastings Cutoff. *See main entry*
  and Lincoln, 18, **19,** 20, 25–26, 37, 134
  and lost oxen, 61–64, 166
  as Mason, 24, 71, 93, 116
  and rescue efforts, 79, 88, 93, 111, 113, **115,**
    116–21, 127, 169–70
  and San Jose, 111, 148
  and Snyder's stabbing, 69–70, 98, 126, 148, 157

Reed, James Frazier, Jr., 24, **149,** 150, 166–67. *See
    also* Reed family

Reed, James Frazier, III, 157–58

Reed, Margaret, 20–22, **21,** 24–26, 29, 32, 56, 63,
    148–50, **149,** 157. *See also* Reed family
  and Graves, Elizabeth, 98, 143

Reed, Martha (Patty or Matty), 24, **25,** 50–52, 61,
    92, 101, 121, 128–29, **128, 138, 149,** 151, 153,
    157, **160, 162,** 167. *See also* Reed family

Reed, Thomas, 24, **149,** 150, 166. *See also* Reed
    family

Reed, Virginia, 17, 20, 23–24, 26–31, 38, 40, 50, 52,
    123, **138,** 139, 144, **152,** 153, 157, 160, **160,**
    182. *See also* Reed family
  and buffalo hunting, 34–35
  in California, 148–52
  and Catholicism, 102, 150–51, 170–71
  death of, 152
  and father, 26, 34, 36, 48, 60, 69–73, 126–27, 151
  and Forlorn Hope, 127, 167–68
  and grandmother's death, 33–34
  and Hastings Cutoff, 48, 52, 56, 126, 159, 163, 170
  letter about Donner Party by, 125–29, **126,** 141,
    148, 150–51, 163, 165–71
  marriage of, 151
  and Native Americans, 31, **38,** 38–39, 167
  and pony Billy, 17, 26, 29–30, 33, 39, 56–57
  thirteenth birthday of, 36

Reed, Willianoski, 149, **149**

Reed family. *See also individual names*
  adopts Donner children, 145–46, 149, **149**